OKAVANGO
Jewel of the Kalahari

KAREN ROSS

PICTURE CREDITS AND COPYRIGHT

Pages 25–40
25 Tim Liversedge; 26 Carol Farneti; 27 top Carol Hughes; 27 bottom left & right, 28 Carol Farneti; 29 top left Karen Ross; 29 top & middle right Tim Liversedge; 29 bottom left & right, 30, 31 Carol Farneti; 32, 33 top George Calef; 33 bottom Bev Joubert; 34, 35 Carol Hughes; 36 George Calef; 37 top Carol Farneti; 37 bottom Bev Joubert; 38, 39 Carol Farneti; 40 George Calef

Pages 49–56
49 Carol Farneti; 50 Teresa Townsend; 51 Karen Ross; 52 Carol Farneti; 53 Jim Clare; 54 George Calef; 55 Carol Farneti; 56 top George Calef; 56 bottom Bev Joubert; 57 George Calef; 58, 59 Carol Farneti; 60 top George Calef; 60 bottom left & middle, 61 Carol Farneti; 62–3, 64 George Calef

Pages 81–96
81 Carol Farneti; 82 George Calef; 83 top Karen Ross; 83 bottom Carol Farneti; 84 Karen Ross; 85 top Carol Farneti; 85 bottom Carol Hughes; 86, 87, 88, 89 top Carol Farneti; 89 bottom Karen Ross; 90 Tim Liversedge; 91 Carol Farneti; 92 Karen Ross; 93 top left & right, bottom left Carol Farneti; 93 bottom right Karen Ross; 94 top Carol Farneti; 94 bottom left & right Karen Ross; 95, 96 top, bottom left Carol Farneti; 96 bottom right Karen Ross.

Pages 113–128
113 Carol Farneti; 114 top Karen Ross; 114 bottom left & right Carol Farneti; 115 Karen Ross; 116, 117, 118 Carol Farneti; 119, 120–121 Karen Ross; 122 Carol Farneti; 123 top Tim Liversedge; 123 bottom Karen Ross; 124 top Carol Farneti; 124 bottom Karen Ross, 125 J Clare; 126 Ian Michler/SIL; 127, 128 top, bottom left Carol Farneti; 128 bottom right Tim Liversedge.

Pages 145–160
145 Karen Ross; 146 Ian Michler/SIL; 147 Carol Farneti; 148–149 Karen Ross; 150, 151 George Calef; 152 top Sally Barrow; 152 bottom, 153 George Calef; 154 top Carol Farneti; 154 bottom left & right Karen Ross; 155 Tim Liversedge; 156, 157 Carol Farneri, 158 George Calef; 159 Carol Hughes; 160 Sally Barrow.

Pages 169–184
169 Jonathan Bowles; 170 top Karen Ross; 170 bottom Carol Farneti; 171 top left Karen Ross; 171l top right, bottom Carol Farneti; 172 Sande Greer; 173 top Tim Liversedge; 173 bottom Sande Greer; 174 Carol Farneti; 175 Sam Miller; 176, 177 top Mike Rosenberg; 177 bottom, 178 top Karen Ross; 178 bottom Carol Farneti; 179 Karen Ross; 180 top Mike Rosenberg; 180 bottom Karen Ross; 181, 182 Carol Farneti; 182 inset Tim Liversedge; 189 Karen Ross; 184 top Carol Farneti; 184 bottom Sally Barrow.

Pages 201–208
All Karen Ross, except 203 Horst Klem; 205 bottom Haraldo Castro/CI; 207 top Lani Asato/CI

Cover picture and spine: Chris Harvey
Backflap: Julian Cook

Struik Publishers
(a division of New Holland Publishing
(South Africa) (Pty) Ltd)
Cornelis Struik House
80 McKenzie Street
Cape Town 8001

New Holland Publishing is a member of the
Johnnic Publishing Group.
www.struik.co.za
Log on to our photographic website
www.imagesofafrica.co.za
for an African experience.

First published in 2003
1 3 5 7 9 10 8 6 4 2

Copyright © published edition:
Struik Publishers, 2003
Copyright © text: Karen Ross, 2003

Publishing manager: Pippa Parker
Managing editor: Helen de Villiers
Editor: Jeanne Hromník
Design director: Janice Evans
Designer: Lesley Mitchell

Reproduction by Hirt & Carter Cape (Pty) Ltd
Printed and bound by Sirivatana Interprint
Public Co Ltd

ISBN 1 86872 729 7

Foreword

When *Okavango – Jewel of the Kalahari* was first published in 1987, Conservation International (CI) was a fledgling yet feisty group with an important mission to protect global biodiversity. CI quickly gained ground with a highly targeted approach that focuses on biodiversity hotspots – 25 places on earth that cover only 1.4 per cent of land surface yet claim more than 60 per cent of all terrestrial species.

CI also threw its energies into the protection of major tropical wilderness areas, which deserve special attention because of their very high levels of species diversity and endemism. A recent analysis identified the miombo-mopane wood-lands and grasslands of southern Africa, which includes the Okavango and Kalahari, as one of the world's top five High Biodiversity Wilderness Areas, along with the three great rainforest areas of Amazonia, New Guinea and the Congo basin.

Karen Ross's passion and commitment are also in a special class. Her book captures the essence of a unique people and the precious place they are struggling to preserve. Karen has a keen understanding of, and compassion for, the local people. A professional conservationist, she is a formidable fighter for the cause.

CI has been at the forefront of the struggle to prevent misguided water projects from diverting the Delta's water and to avert another extreme threat – that from wildlife fences built to comply with EU disease control regulations. CI believes the Okavango region is a crucial piece of a huge megacorridor that encompasses part of Botswana, Namibia, Angola, Zimbabwe and Zambia and includes the largest elephant popu-lations on earth. We also believe that the region merits recognition as a World Heritage Site.

CI will continue to work with Botswana's leadership, with partner organisations, and with the people of the Okavango who for centuries have made the Delta their home. We are focus-ing on ways to increase local communities' benefits from the natural riches that the Delta provides, with special emphasis on ecotourism. Together, we can ensure that this biological jewel remains vibrantly alive.

Peter A Seligmann, Chairman & CEO, and
Russell A Mittermeier, President.
CONSERVATION INTERNATIONAL, WASHINGTON DC

Contents

Maps

Acknowledgements

firstly I wish to thank Botswana, the people and their country, for providing my family with a special home and the opportunity to work in and for their stunning wetland, the Okavango.

This book first came out as a companion to the BBC series of the same name, produced by Michael Rosenberg of Partridge Films. The series won Mike the prestigious BBC Golden Panda Award in 1988. The videos are still available, and are a wonderful guide to this remarkable place. Many of the photographs in the book came from the filming of the series and I wish to take this opportunity to thank all the photographers who contributed. Their names are listed opposite.

Special thanks to the many colleagues and friends of Conservation International worldwide, particularly in the Botswana and Cape Town offices – it has been a treat to work with you under the inspiring leadership of Peter Seligmann and Russ Mittermier, who kindly wrote the foreword to this edition. I also wish to acknowledge Allan Thornton who led the Greenpeace mission to Botswana; Ted Skudder the team leader of the IUCN survey of the SOIWDP project, and Peter-John Meynell who led the Environmental Impact Assessment of Ngamiland fences. It is a privilege to work with you.

There are, of course, new people to thank from the years since this book first came out, especially those families with whom my daughter, Lena Rae, and I shared the fun and the ups and downs of growing up. There are many to cherish, but in particular we wish to thank the Peak, Raitt, Thouless, Longdon, McNeice, Leaver, Quinnlivan, Nixon, Harvey, Cook, Rawson, Dugmore, Watson, Mavros/McDonald families. Much love to you all.

Thanks to the Batemans, Marshalls, Sheldons and Collingwoods in Gaborone for their hospitality and to Colin Craig and Debbie Gibson in Windhoek. And thank you to many special friends, too many to mention, who have enriched my life so much: my soul sister Leslie Sundt, Ian Ross and Mark Marshall who helped to keep me flying, and my guides Kumi and Colin Campbell. And Sande Greer – a great father to Lena and the man who, not least, introduced roller hockey to Botswana.

I am fortunate to have had friends and donors without whom the conservation work described here would not have been possible – businesses, foundations, bi-lateral donors and the Board of Conservation International, as well as individuals. Thanks to you all, especially Maggie Bryant, John Laing, Herb Allan, Vincent Mai, Roger Altman and Charles Mayhew, for your unstinting support. You are champions of conservation.

Always, through thick and thin, our family has been there for us: as ever, Mum and Dad; my brother, Paul Ross, who taught me to fly, and his family Franca and Marco; and my lovely sister, June Vetch, and her family, Stewart, Cynara and Liana. Thanks and love to you all.

Struik Publishers have been fantastic. Many thanks to the entire production team, especially commissioning editor Pippa Parker and design director Janice Evans. And editor Jeanne Hromnik who worked tirelessly and with such enthusiasm on this new edition.

Finally, love to you, Lena, and thanks for your help in re-editing this book – you are a joy and a truly wonderful daughter.

In Memoriam

This book is dedicated to the memory of the many friends and colleagues with whom I was fortunate to have shared time in this special part of the world.

Jack Bousfield
Rick Lomba
Charlie Raitt
Pete Smith
Richard Bell
Moremi Sekwale
Modise Mothoagae
Neville Peake
Alistair Torr
Struin
Nicky Wright
Alison McGill
Elly Gordon Brown
Silver

Author's Note

When I wrote *Jewel of the Kalahari* in the eighties I didn't imagine that I would spend the next decade and more living, breathing and fighting for the Okavango, not to mention falling in love, marrying and raising a child there! Well, not all in the Delta itself, but mainly in Maun, the small, dusty frontier town that is the last stop before the bush. Luckily, I have been given the chance to republish the book and call attention to the threats and opportunities that are playing out on the Okavango's natural stage.

In my early days there, the only road access to Maun was along 300 kilometres of deep, rutted track. Only 4x4 vehicles could manage the sand tracks into and through town. The local pub, the Duck Inn, was like a Wild West saloon, with safari trucks parked outside like a line of horses tethered at the rail while, inside, hunters and safari operators shook off the loneliness of the bush with parties and drinking. Isolation made Maun a close-knit but wild place with few modern amenities such as television and telephones.

A tar road, completed in 1993, has replaced the dusty track to Maun. It has attracted more people and, with them, cars and modern needs. From a frontier post with only four outside telephone lines, the town has progressed to the latest microwave telecommunications; the telephone pages for Maun have increased from one to ten. Many have cell phones. A small but modern airport has replaced the tiny airport shack, enlarged to take passenger aircraft including a daily flight from Johannesburg and another from Botswana's capital, Gaborone.

As if to signal the passing of an era, the Duck Inn closed. My daughter, Lena Rae, with whom I was pregnant when I wrote *Jewel of the Kalahari* is now a teenager. People grow and so do places. In essence, however, Maun is the same. If you scratch the surface, beneath is the same frontier outpost – tough and gritty, hot and dusty.

Just as Maun has grown, so the Okavango has changed – not so much from the pressures of a livelier and more populous town, but because of a wide range of very real environmental dangers. Water extraction, cattle fences and farming are but a few. Numerous opportunities have arisen, however, out of the efforts of people to preserve the Okavango and their heritage.

With Maun's greater accessibility, tourism and hunting in the Okavango have flourished to the point where concern is being voiced about over-crowding this delicate ecosystem. In an effort to lighten the human footprint, the Botswana authorities have wisely favoured high-cost, low-volume tourism. Tourists are flown in small planes to camps discreetly hidden in the bush, where vehicles are few.

The Okavango River traverses three nations: it rises in Angola, flows through Namibia and empties onto the Kalahari sands of Botswana. The river's delta lies at the lower end of the river basin, and being so positioned is at the mercy of upstream users. In any event, water extraction from a wetland in an arid sub-continent, where summer temperatures are extreme and annual evaporation is 95 per cent of inflow, is guaranteed to have a substantial impact. Battles over water will always be a part of the Okavango's existence.

When first written, the last chapter of this book raised the spectre of an imminent threat to the Delta – a water-extraction project popularly known as 'the Boro dredging'. Between the pro-ponents of the project and the local community there ensued a bitter battle, which was won at the last moment. Since then the Namibian master plan to supply Windhoek with water from the Okavango has been successfully chal-lenged. A large-scale threat to the Delta has now arisen from a proposed Namibian hydro-electric scheme on the Popa Falls in Caprivi.

Botswana has a controversial history of fence construction. Much remains to be done to open up important wildlife corridors by the realignment or removal of key fences, but even in this thorny issue heartening progress has been made. A fences committee involving government and conservation groups was formed and, as a result, a crucial wildlife corridor was opened. Botswana recently commissioned its first ever environmental impact study of fences – its recommendations, if followed, will reduce significantly the impact of fences on wildlife.

Conservation International has been active in the region for over a decade, working with numerous groups including local communities. Signifcant international funding is in process, and the three river basin states are now collaborat-ing in the formulation of an Okavango River Basin Treaty, the first of its kind in Africa.

During my time in the Okavango I have seen people change the course of history. Indeed there is a growth of spirit and energy worldwide – increased awareness and collective conscious-ness. One has only to listen to young people today (an insight also conveyed to me by my daughter) to know that there is hope for the future. Important environmental battles have been fought, and won, in the Okavango. They have taught me about the power of community to make a difference and the ability of the human spirit to influence destiny. As the Okavango successes suggest, people may be a cause of the problem, but they are also a part of the solution.

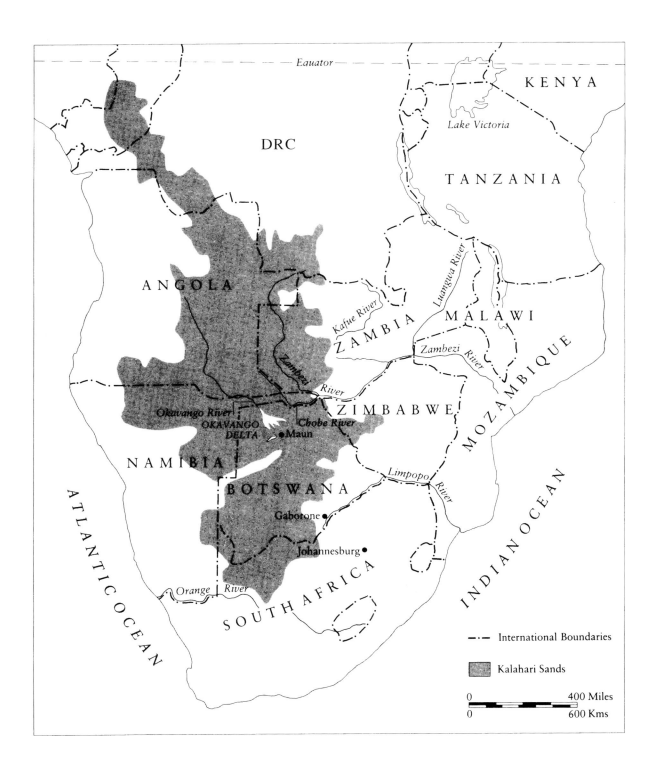

CHAPTER ONE

Sands of a Continent

from a bird's eye view, high in the pale cloudless sky, the land stretches for ever. Awash with browns and yellows, there is no visible water to reflect the sun and bring a sparkle to the landscape. At this height the wilderness is frighteningly flat, almost dreary; on the horizon you can see the curve of the earth as it dips beyond view.

The heat from the ground creates thermals which keep the martial eagle soaring, its wings motionless as it circles and searches for food. What life is there in this emptiness? A movement catches the eagle's eye and it swoops lower. On a hot sun-baked mound a watchful suricate screeches a warning. There is a frantic flurry of skinny bodies, long tails and blonde fur as the look-out's companions make a dash for the communal burrow. Thwarted, the eagle flies off. Catching a thermal, it soars once again over its domain – the Kalahari.

In their burrow, the suricates, a type of mongoose also called meerkats, hug each other and twitter and chatter. In a second they are out and foraging again, digging in the sand for scorpions and beetles, only half aware of the danger from the skies because they have a guard to watch for them on a rise in their otherwise flat territory. Standing on its hind legs the look-out stares at the sky, its distinctive black belly and highwayman mask offering protection from the searing sun. Suricates have evolved a way of dealing with the harsh life of the Kalahari; amongst the most sociable creatures on earth, they depend on one another for safety and food and for help when needed.

This is the central Kalahari, in the heart of southern Africa. Sand dominates the landscape, which stretches for hundreds of miles without surface water except after rain – and here rain is fickle. Sand is perhaps one of nature's harshest habitats. Like a sponge it sucks and drains any water that touches its surface. Over millennia this gradual seepage of water has taken nutrients with it, leaving a sandy soil baked by the sun.

The coarse grains of sand are a harsh and gritty medium in which it is difficult to live and move about. They reflect the heat of the sun mercilessly and, unless stabilised by vegetation, are carried away by wind. Life is here, however, in surprising diversity. Plants and animals have developed wonderful ways of coping with the heavy heat of summer, the icy cold of winter and the harshness of the Kalahari.

The increase in rainfall across its expanse from south to north changes the vegetation. In the south, where the Kalahari is truly arid, ochre-red dunes and wide 'rivers' of sand dominate the landscape. In the central region a slightly higher rainfall supports acacia grasslands, which merge into the deciduous woodlands, rivers and swamps of the north.

Our story is set in the central Kalahari, in the northern part of Botswana. This is a transition zone, a land of anomalies, where the sands are covered by the Okavango Delta, an expanse of fresh blue water and floating emerald islands of reeds. Beside the Delta are the dry remnants of the ancient Lake Makgadikgadi. It is here that the 'desert' displays its most astonishing diversity.

Notwithstanding this variety of landscapes, the Kalahari has one defining feature: a flat blanket cover of thick sand. Geologically, it is a huge sand-filled basin – the largest continuous stretch of sand in the world, covering some 2 500 kilometres in the heart of southern Africa from the Orange (Gariep) River in South Africa northwards to the tropical forests of the DRC (Democratic Republic of the Congo). During its formation the Kalahari has undergone great changes, many of them only recently discovered. There is tantalising evidence that this was once a lush area covered by sub-tropical forests, wide rivers and huge lakes.

Origins of the Kalahari

The origins of the Kalahari go back 135 million years. At this time the southern 'super-continent' of Gondwanaland was beginning to break up, giving birth to Africa as a continent. Reptiles were the dominant animals on earth, having followed the evolution of insects, fish and amphibians. Mammals were tiny nocturnal creatures, hiding from the predatory dinosaurs that roamed the ancient super-continent.

Gondwanaland was destined to form the world's southern continents. It consisted of a series of tectonic plates (huge sections of the earth's crust) which began to drift apart, each carrying its own selection of animal and plant life. India and Madagascar were first to sever their connection; then Antarctica and Australia broke away from the south-east side of Africa. Perhaps a million years later South America moved off westwards.

By 100 million years ago Africa stood alone as a continent, much the shape it is today. Soon after its isolation, much of Africa was uplifted by the inner rumblings of the earth. In the interior of the continent great basins were formed – Chad to the north, the Congo basin in central Africa, the Kalahari to the south. For 60 million years, the landscape was relatively peaceful. High areas were gradually worn down by the relentless activity of water, ice, heat and wind, and the basins slowly filled. It was during this period that the Kalahari basin received the sands of the continent.

12

Africa did not cease to move after it had become a separate land mass. The continent drifted southwards, and its climate became increasingly dry. This resulted in changes in the Kalahari's vegetation, sub-tropical forests giving way to thorny scrub and plants that still occur in the Kalahari today. Since there were no major land barriers in the region, birds and larger mammals migrated from north and south, creating an even greater diversity of animal life.

Some 30 million years ago, a long period of stability and gentle erosion was disrupted by violent activity. The giant continent was finally awake; Africa was rocked, buckled and broken. A series of great rifts were formed, stretching almost 5 000 kilometres from the Red Sea along the east of the continent and ending just north of the Kalahari. At these rifts the tectonic plates were drifting apart, in a process similar to that in which Gondwanaland broke up. The earth's crust was stretched and thinned, resulting in volcanic activity along the lines of stress. The rifts, volcanoes and uplifts raised the landscape to new heights, restricting the passage of moist air from the north and creating even more arid conditions in southern Africa.

The climate of the Kalahari was made still drier by the glaciation of an ancient neighbour, Antarctica. As this continent moved towards the South Pole and completed its glaciation, about five million years ago, cold sea currents and air flows iced over the huge continent, sucking up moisture and bringing drought and dryness.

With the arrival of intense aridity, strong winds spread the Kalahari's sand mantle widely and evenly. During this period plants and animals evolved the remarkable adaptations that enable them to withstand long periods of drought.

Rivers of sand

About three million years ago the Kalahari was truly arid. Strong easterly winds blew the sands into long dunes orientated east to west, running in parallel ridges. These dunes influenced the flow of rivers during the wetter times that followed, contributing to a remarkable event: the Kalahari's sands were to form one of the largest lakes that Africa has seen, Lake Makgadikgadi. The Okavango Delta is the last remnant of this ancient lake.

The sand dunes are now stabilised by vegetation. Depressions between the ridges catch water run-off from the infrequent rains, forming wide 'fossil valleys' – the ancient remnants of rivers that once carried huge volumes of water across a wetter Kalahari. Even now these old valleys act as drainage channels and, although they are rivers of sand for most of the year, beneath their surface flows subterranean water. Among the few plants that can tap this deep water source is the camelthorn acacia, which grows along the the banks of fossil valleys, sending roots 30 metres into the sand to reach underground water. Occasionally a grove of dead trees indicates a place where the water table has dropped below reach of their roots.

Trees that give life

The camelthorn is a valuable tree. Its leaves, flowers and pods are an important source of food and the canopy provides shelter from the fierce heat for all manner of creatures, from the desert agama lizard to the Kalahari lion. Plants, too, profit from the shade: more nutritious grasses than in the surrounding sandveldt grow in this cooler, moister place, which is enriched by nitrogen-fixing microbes in the roots of acacias.

Every year the landscape is graced by the yellow pom-pom flowers of the camelthorn and the massed purple blossoms of the rain tree, attracting and feeding pollinating insects. The showy flowers usually signal rain, but often they come and go and the rains do not arrive. Perhaps their appearance is triggered by increasing day length rather than the promise of rain.

At the onset of the Kalahari summer in October the camelthorn produces hundreds of thick half-moon-shaped pods. These pods, unlike those of most acacias, do not split to scatter their seeds. Instead, animals eat the pods and the seeds are passed out of their digestive tracts unharmed and are so dispersed. Larger animals such as giraffes and gemsboks relish the pods as a rich food source. This is the tree's way of encouraging the spread of its seeds.

However, not all creatures act as harmless seed-dispersers. Rodents feed on the seeds themselves. The pouched mouse, a charming, slow-moving creature that does not linger long outside its burrow, gnaws through camelthorn pods and collects the seeds in the pouches of its cheeks. Carrying seeds and insects collected on its foraging trip, the mouse returns to its burrow to eat at leisure and in safety.

With the camelthorn comes a host of creatures such as acacia rats, social weaver birds and bushbabies that use it. Lesser bushbabies, also known as galagos, are endearing little creatures with huge eyes that help night vision. They spend their lives in trees, where they nest in hollows or disused birds' nests, supplementing their staple food of insects with the gum of acacias, an important part of their diet in the dry season.

Although bushbabies tend to forage alone they are highly social, with over 25 vocal sounds such as grunts, clicks, twitters and chatters. Their ability to turn their heads through 180 degrees compensates for being unable to move their eyeballs within the socket. Bushbabies moisten their hands with urine to mark their territory but also to help get a purchase as they leap from branch to branch with spectacular bounds. They grab with long fingers at insect prey as it flies past and eat it rather like an ice-cream cone.

The shepherd's tree is able to survive in this harsh land and provides food, water and shelter. Its flowers are rich in honey and many creatures, from pied babblers to black-backed jackals, eat the summer berries. In older trees the wizened trunks collect rainwater, traditionally an important source of desert water for Bushmen. These beautifully-adapted trees are a lifeline in the Kalahari and, not surprisingly, a protected species.

Sun-bleached grasses

A wilderness of sun-bleached grasses sparsely covers the sands of the central Kalahari. In the scorching noonday heat only the wind whispers and stirs the golden blades. Stunted thickets of blackthorn acacia dot the savanna, interspersed by shrubs and herbs that blossom only briefly after rain. Their harvest lies buried beneath the sand – roots and underground tubers swollen with moisture. As the Kalahari dried, woodlands receded northwards and grasses took their place.

Searing heat and the unpredictability of rain compound the difficulties of life in sand. In some years, heavy rains can transform the land into a carpet of green grass interspersed by flushes of jewel-like flowers. They may be followed by years of drought. To survive, plants and animals have had to compromise in their adaptations. Plants need sunshine to grow, but sunshine desiccates. Animals must feed, but lose water in so doing. Those that survive, not surprisingly, are those that have found a balance.

Grasses are vital to life here: their leaves and roots provide food and nesting material, seeds are eaten by insects, rodents and birds. They have extensive root systems that spread out to trap moisture and by so doing stabilise sand that would otherwise snake and shift unhindered across the land. Many send out short-lived roots during the rains to maximise the uptake of water. The roots of perennial grasses are often encased in a sand sheath that protects them from the drying effect of the soil. Even here, under good

grass cover subterranean moisture from rain may last for many months, held in the sand.

Most grasses are annuals, growing quickly and setting seed at the onset of the cold dry season in May, seeds being better able to withstand the long drought. In winter the grass is killed by frost and the seeds lie dormant, but they germinate quickly with the arrival of the rains. Some grasses deter grazing animals with leaves that are covered in gland-tipped hairs which, when eaten, release a sticky blistering exudate.

Some seeds have evolved ingenious methods of reproduction. Kalahari plume grass has feathery, white seed-heads that stick and twist themselves into the sand the moment there is sufficient moisture so that they cannot be blown away when ready to germinate. For most seeds, however, wind is the agent of dispersal, blowing them across the sands until they encounter a ridge or clump of vegetation that halts their random scattering. To prevent growth after a freak shower, some seeds have chemicals that inhibit germination until enough water has washed them away.

Seeds are an abundant and important food source for insects, rodents and birds. The cone-headed katydid, an exotic type of grasshopper, has powerful jaws that can crack open grass seeds. The desert pygmy mouse, a tiny nocturnal rodent that occurs widely in Kalahari grasslands, depends on grasses for food. It takes refuge in a shallow burrow in the sand during the day and builds a ball-shaped nest of soft grass.

Desert adaptations

Although many birds in the central Kalahari are seed-eaters, few eat seeds exclusively because seeds contain so little water. Those that do, such as the namaqua dove and double-banded sandgrouse, must drink regularly. This restricts their distribution since standing water is rare. The majority of birds, including most larks and the social weavers, obtain additional moisture by eating insects. Termites are a good moisture-providing food source.

Among the Kalahari's most striking birds is the kori bustard, the world's heaviest flying bird. In the Kalahari its relative, the red-crested korhaan, performs a spectacular flight display: it flies upwards like a wound-up toy, tumbles over with plumage fluffed and opens its wings like a parachute just before landing. These birds are among those that supplement their seed diet with insects as well as acacia gum. The diet of successful birds in the Kalahari involves both compromise and flexibility.

Smaller plants such as mesembryanthemums and aloes retain moisture in their leaves, and animals make use of this store of water. More than 50 species of animals and birds have been recorded visiting a single aloe plant in the Kalahari. Mesembryanthemums have ingenious dispersal mechanisms to ensure their survival. When ripe, their seed pods are blown across the sand by the wind, remaining closed until rain dissolves the valves of the pods and the seeds can germinate.

Wild species of cucumber and tsama melons encase their yearly production of seeds in succulent, water-filled fruits used by many creatures, from porcupines to brown hyaenas, for food and water. Some plants grow large tubers beneath the sand that store water for the plant in times of drought, a useful source of food as well as water. Sand is a perfect medium for the unhindered growth of these tubers.

The morama bulb or gemsbok bean grows to a great size – one was found that weighed 260 kilograms and contained 200 litres of water. The grapple-plant is of commercial value as it contains a chemical that is one of the few known treatments for arthritis. Its name comes from the bizarre seed with its gin-trap device for clasping the foot of a passing creature, thereby ensuring dispersal.

The animals of the Kalahari know the secrets of this underground feast, which is available even in the driest times. So too do Bushmen hunter-gatherers who survive in this inhospitable land by using more than 200 species of edible plants, turning to different food sources in changing seasons. They have favourites among them, such as underground truffles similar to the delicacies that grow in the oak forests of France.

The oldest inhabitants

Insects, frogs and reptiles are the oldest inhabitants of the Kalahari. Termites, which play such a vital role in the ecology of the Kalahari, existed 100 million years ago, their body form showing no apparent differences from that of termites today. The termite mound is probably one of the earliest types of organised community on earth.

To avoid extremes of temperature and retain moisture harvester termites situate their nests deep in the ground. The home of a vigorous colony may consist of 20 or so nests connected by a complex system of winding tunnels. In the cold winters annual grasses die off and are of little nutritive value, but they are food for harvester termites, which in turn provide succulent termite flesh for other creatures. In this way termites are at the base of a massive food web that sustains the Kalahari's creatures, including larger mammals such as aardvarks and aardwolves.

In the intense heat of summer harvester termites are active at night, but in winter, when night-time temperatures can drop below freezing point, they forage by day. Their heads are covered by a horny brown skin to protect them from the sun's glare, unlike the translucent skin of the nocturnal 'fungus termite'. The small holes through which the workers emerge to forage are the only surface evidence of harvester termite colonies, but keen eyes soon detect their comings and goings. Indeed, when termites are busy, hornbills flock to the ground, pick up the delectable creatures with their large beaks and toss them down their throats. Black pomerine ants can overpower and carry away solitary termite workers.

When their enemies become too numerous the harvesters descend to their subterranean colony, blocking up the holes as they retreat.

Narrow branching tunnels underground lead downwards into the earth to cellars where they live, surrounded by their store of food. Here, in coolness and safety, the coarse dry grass of the sandveldt is processed. Eaten and partly digested, it is fed to others and thus converted into termite protein.

While larger creatures sink and labour in the deep sands, the lesser creatures of the Kalahari are at home. In a fascinating array of body designs, skin textures and colour patterns, they run over sand, dive through it and generally thrive in this dry, gritty and abrasive medium. One way or another they are able to use sand – to escape the heat, avoid water loss, hide from an enemy or to lie in wait for prey.

The larvae of dragonfly-like antlion insects use their sandy homes to trap insects, their small pits a common sight in sandy areas across Africa. The small grub-like larva lives at the bottom of the pit. When a passing insect disturbs a few grains of sand the waiting antlion is alerted and quickly tosses sand at the insect with its head, making it slip down the steep sides of the sandy cone. The insect finally falls to the bottom, where it is grasped by the powerful claws of the antlion and dragged beneath the sand.

Some spiders make use of sand grains to help trap their prey. The back-flip spider digs a small hollow and incorporates sand grains into its web to disguise it. Once the web is constructed, the spider flips over on its back and pulls the web over itself, waiting for prey to become entangled.

Beetles are the most common insect group in the Kalahari. Fossils from the central Kalahari dated back 95 million years show that beetles were the most common insects even then. As a group, tenebrionid beetles, which are found in arid regions throughout the world, show some of the finest adaptations to life in sand. Some are able to 'swim' through sand because of their flattened body shape; others have a remarkable ability to store water.

Anthia beetles, black with yellow dots and stripes on the body, are ferocious hunters with powerful pincer-like jaws. They squirt formic acid at potential troublemakers. The juvenile Kalahari sand lizard mimics the noxious *Anthia*. Adult lizards are yellow and brown, but the colour of the juveniles are strikingly different – black with yellow markings, like the beetle. The mimicry extends to movement: adult sand lizards walk with a normal lizard gait, their bodies swaying from side to side, whereas juveniles walk stiff-legged with arched backs. Should the deception fail, the 'beetle walk' is abandoned and the young dash for cover! Surveys show that the number of broken tails among juvenile Kalahari sand lizards is lower than among closely-related lizards, suggesting that the mimicry works.

Reptiles have superb adaptations to arid environments. They reproduce independently of water and their skin is largely resistant to water loss. Most Kalahari lizards have long, webbed toes and streamlined bodies that move easily over sand. When the surface becomes scorchingly hot they stand on alternate pairs of legs, keeping the other two legs raised and cool in a lovely manoeuvre called 'thermal dancing'.

Snakes, the last of the great reptile groups to evolve, have taken the legless-lizard concept to an elegant extreme. With their impermeable skins and slender body shape they can overcome the problems posed by an arid sandy habitat. Some Kalahari snakes, such as blind snakes and worm snakes, a primitive group almost as closely related to lizards as they are to snakes, live below ground. Usually associated with termite mounds, these snakes have a short blunt head, covered by a shield and highly polished scales, which makes it easier to burrow. Among them is the shield-nosed snake, beautifully coloured in black and coral tones.

Although it resembles the harmless burrowing snakes, the burrowing adder is a deadly predator. Its small head restricts normal striking; instead, it retracts its lower jaw to reveal flattened fangs, which strike their prey sideways – an effective way of catching lizards and rodents in narrow underground passages.

Burrowing is a technique also used by the small mammals of the Kalahari to conserve water and keep cool. Rodents, the most numerous of the Kalahari's small mammals, excavate burrows deep below the surface. To minimise water loss they are often nocturnal. Bushveldt gerbils live in colonies deep below the sand, the entrance usually beside a clump of vegetation to stabilise the sand. Their burrowing activities and droppings create richer soil which plants can colonise and their cool moist burrows are shared with scorpions, millipedes and beetles.

A long sleep

In a prolonged drought Kalahari creatures resort to other tactics. Some move away in search of food, and birds can fly away, but the smaller animals can do neither. Hence, many aestivate until conditions get better. This is the arid-land equivalent of hibernation – a long sleep when the body just ticks over, using little energy and avoiding stress. Amphibians are by nature dependent on water, but some frogs are able to survive through aestivation.

The Kalahari burrowing frog's life-cycle restricts it to a subterranean life unless it rains. Special fluids and a large bladder enable it to store and recycle water while it aestivates. This fascinating little frog is only a few centimetres long with a fat round body, tiny head and small feet. It cannot jump or even swim. The male's fat tummy and short arms make it impossible for him to embrace a female. Instead he exudes a white glue to attach himself to her. It must be a superglue for the pair then dig into the soil, slowly revolving backwards into the earth where they find a suitable spot to excavate a cavity in which the female lays her eggs. How the pair becomes unglued is a mystery.

CHAPTER TWO

Realm of the Unicorn

the large animals of the Kalahari also exhibit ingenious behaviours and clever designs that enable them to survive. Although water-dependent animals such as zebras and elephants sometimes wander the grasslands of the central Kalahari, only those that can survive without drinking water may be considered true residents of the arid interior, where there is no standing water except after rain and the rains are fickle. The Kalahari has become increasingly dry over millennia; droughts are the norm and wet years are exceptional.

This is the realm of the gemsbok, a large antelope of the oryx family whose beauty is matched by superb adaptations to desert life. Both sexes have dramatic black face stripes and carry long rapier-sharp horns which provide a lethal defence against all predators, even lions. The glossy silver-grey coat reflects and helps dissipate heat. Gemsboks have remarkable adaptations to water scarcity. By allowing their body temperature to increase rather than lose precious water by sweating, they can tolerate temperatures up to 45^{0}C, which would kill other mammals. The blood flowing to the gemsbok's brain along the

arteries is cooled by a network of veins in the nasal passage. Cooler blood carried in these veins reduces the temperature of the arterial blood to around 42^{0}C – the maximum the brain can tolerate without damage. By breathing more deeply rather than more rapidly, the animal is able to increase the air flow over its fine nasal veins and so minimise water loss.

The traditional life of Bushmen reflects the value of the gemsbok. When a young girl enters womanhood, a gemsbok is killed and she wears a cap made of its stomach. This keeps her young and strong for of all the Kalahari's animals the gemsbok is said to carry its years best.

Only a handful of antelopes can survive without water: they include gemsboks, springboks, greater kudus, red hartebeests and elands. Like all antelopes they are ruminants, with an extra stomach to digest plant material with which ordinary stomach acids cannot cope, and it is only through careful choice of habitat and flexible feeding behaviour that they can survive without moisture. Each species has its place within the small variations of topography and vegetation overlying the blanket of Kalahari sand.

The basic habitats of Kalahari antelopes are sand dunes and ancient drainage points (fossil valleys, dry water-holes and lake beds) and flat sandy plateaux. The sides of valleys are lined with sandy banks which rise into sand-dune ridges. The shallow pans – dry lake beds for most of the year – often have a dune on one side. This is formed by the prevailing wind, which scoops up sand from the pan floor, thereby maintaining both pan and dune.

Plants that store their food and moisture reserves underground thrive in the loose sandy soils of the dunes. Trees, such as the camelthorn acacia, the silver terminalia and the leadwood tree, send their roots deep into the sand to tap underground water. Thus, somewhat surprisingly, sand dunes are capped with woodlands of shady trees, overlooking the tawny long grass and thornveldt of the surrounding plateau and the short grass of the pans and winding valleys.

Pans and dry river valleys have a higher clay content than the sands of the dunes and plateaux since the water draining into these depressions has deposited clay particles and organic matter over millennia. The clay slows the drainage of water after rain, temporarily providing animals with areas of standing water. The difference in soil and drainage also has an effect on the vegetation. Because of seasonal water-logging, trees do not grow on the pan and valley floors, which support short grasses instead. Owing to differences in water-storage capacities between sand and clay, the heavier clay soils dry

faster than the arid dunes. Dune woodlands are, therefore, important to animals in the dry season. Juxtaposed, however, the two habitats offer a surprisingly wide variety of food and cover to animals, which move from one to the other according to the changing seasons.

The trees and shrubs of the sand dunes provide sustenance throughout the year for browsing animals such as the giraffe and kudu. Steenboks – small desert-adapted antelopes with large rabbit-like ears which help dissipate heat – also inhabit the wooded dune crests. They are solitary creatures that live all year round in well-marked territories, protecting their precious food resources rather than moving to new grazing areas as many of the Kalahari's antelopes do.

Elands, on the other hand, are highly mobile, ranging over huge areas in their search for food, switching their diet from grass to shrubs as conditions demand. Red hartebeests wander the thornveldt of the plains, browsing on small bushes and grasses and digging for tubers in the dry season.

Kalahari pans

Pans scattered throughout the Kalahari are an important characteristic of the area. There are salt pans, rock pans and clay pans, and they vary in size from depressions a few hundred metres across to dry lake beds several kilometres wide. They are richer in minerals, salts and water than other areas and have a marked effect on animal movements. The presence of mineral-rich pans may explain why the more water-dependent creatures, such as wildebeests, leave the security of permanent rivers to venture deep into the harsh interior.

The sands of the Kalahari are generally unfertile, and are particularly low in essential minerals such as phosphorus and nitrogen. Most plants and animals that survive are able to compensate for this shortage of nutrients. Herbs of the pea family and some trees of the acacia group are able to supply their own nitrogen fertiliser. Micro-organisms in their roots extract nitrogen from the atmosphere and make it available to the plant, while enriching the soils and the grasses growing amongst them. Antelopes obtain additional phosphorus and calcium by chewing the bones of other animals – also a common practice amongst Africa's largest rodents – porcupines.

Grasses growing on the clay soils of pans and valleys are naturally higher in minerals than the plants of the sandveldt. After rain the pans are covered by a few centimetres of shallow water, which attracts a great variety and number of birds and other animals. The water sometimes lasts for a few days, although in deep pans it might persist for a month or more if it rains again. As the water is evaporated by the sun, moisture containing the salts and minerals of the earth seeps up to replace it. When the last of the moisture evaporates the salts are deposited on the surface, where animals can obtain them. Springboks have the astonishing ability to drink water so salty that it is lethal to most species.

After rain pans and valleys are the focal point for large concentrations of antelopes, which in turn attract predators. Lions wait in the thick bush on the pan edge or dune slope, ready to hunt the antelopes. In the heat of summer most animals spend the day in the shade of dune woodlands, moving to the treeless pans at dusk to feed through the night. Without a cloud blanket in the sky the heat of the sand is quickly lost at night and with the dropping temperature, the humidity of the air increases until its dew-point is reached. Plant cells soak up the dew, even in the leaves of frost- or drought-killed grasses. Both plants and animals benefit from this nightly harvest of water.

At dusk, the calls of barking geckos resound over the sandveldt. These are the calls of territorial males announcing the night with their sharp barks from the entrance to their sandy burrows, the shape of which amplifies sound. The Kalahari is at its most beautiful in the twilight, just before darkness falls and the sandveldt, so barren by day, gradually comes alive with the creatures of the night.

Gemsboks and springboks

Gemsboks and springboks move daily from the dunes to the pans and valleys, seeking the shade of the wooded dunes during the day, moving to the open treeless pans and valleys to feed in the cool of late afternoon. In addition, they move seasonally in response to the changing availability of food and the need for additional moisture.

When the land is green, both gemsboks and springboks generally prefer the short grass of the pans and valleys, where they concentrate after rain. Gemsboks seek cover in the wooded dunes if they are aware of predators; springboks on the other hand will move to the centre of the open areas if they sense danger.

When conditions are dry the pans and valleys are no longer such suitable habitats as their grasses dry more quickly than those on the dunes and plains. In the dry season, gemsboks disperse over the dune crests to search for tubers and underground food, which they dig with their sharp hooves. Springboks also disperse during the dry season although they dig less and browse more than gemsboks, perhaps because of their less powerful build. Since most Kalahari grasses retain some food value even when dry, this switch in the dry season to browsing the shoots, leaves and flowers of herbs and bushes must be linked to satisfying the animals' moisture requirements.

Adult male gemsboks are territorial, which gives them the right to mate with females in the area. Female gemsboks wander in small mixed groups of a dozen or so individuals, covering an annual range of 100 to 200 square kilometres that encompasses the territories of many males. These ranges are small when compared to those of elands, hartebeests or wildebeests in the Kalahari. Gemsboks are so well adapted that they can meet their survival needs in a relatively small area, even in times of severe drought.

They benefit from a limited but familiar range where they know how to meet their needs.

Springboks are smaller and differ in many ways from gemsboks. They are gregarious, moving in small herds in dry periods but forming huge concentrations after rain, when many herds are drawn together. Rain may occur in a particular area once in a decade, but springboks have the mobility to reach it when the rain falls. Their migratory instinct is so strong that once on the move nothing will stop them.

Male springboks mate at all times and the sprouting of green grass is the only environmental trigger or 'cue' that females need to come into breeding condition. Springboks differ thus from seasonal breeders such as impalas and can be opportunistic about when to reproduce. They have a short gestation period of 24 weeks, and, when conditions are favourable, 'lamb' twice in a year. In optimal conditions their offspring reach puberty in six months – compared with two years for most antelopes.

This ability to respond quickly to good conditions resulted in a remarkable build up in numbers of springboks. There are records from the last century of treks of thousands of sprinboks over the arid plains of the Cape. Perhaps they moved in search of rain and fresh pastures or, perhaps, their numbers had grown so great that there was an undeniable instinct to disperse. Great treks occurred four times in the last century, with estimates of their numbers ranging from half a million to 100 million.

'Stotting', also called 'pronking', is a method of locomotion springboks employ when alarmed. (Small antelopes, such as oribi and Thompson's gazelle and even the bat-eared fox, also stot.) It consists of a bounding leap, with back arched and all four legs held stiff. The animal lands on all four legs simultaneously and immediately springs up again with a fan of white back-hairs fully erect, bouncing along like a child on a pogo stick. Stotting may be a ritualised leap that warns others of danger. It is also a method of moving that conserves energy, enabling the springbok to look around and pinpoint a predator while moving away. If a predator singles out an individual and the chase begins, the alarmed springbok abandons the 'stotting' locomotion and tries to escape at full speed.

Unusual predators

The Kalahari has many unusual predators with the typical adaptations of desert creatures: they rest in the heat of day, emerge at night to search for food and are flexible in what they eat. Generally these carnivores are independent of drinking water.

The silver fox, a shy animal, hides during the day in the thick stands of grass on acacia grasslands, well camouflaged by its silver-grey and gold-flecked fur. At dusk it emerges to forage alone, peaks of activity occurring around sunset and sunrise. Silver foxes are avid diggers, scratching out sand-dwelling reptiles such as barking geckos as well as their preferred prey of rodents, especially the slow-moving pouched mouse. Like other Kalahari carnivores they are opportunistic, feeding on insects, birds, berries and even vegetation. They forage alone except when the female has a litter of pups.

The black-backed (also called the silver-backed) jackal is especially abundant in the arid regions of the Kalahari. While barking geckos call at night in summer, the territorial cry of jackals, particularly when females are on heat, is a haunting sound on winter nights. Jackal pairs mate for life, rearing their young in disused aardvark holes. The formation of a strong pair bond ensures that there is always a mate to help in hunting, scavenging and raising the young. The jackal pair are often helped by the grown-up young of the previous litter, which improves the pups' chances of survival. They show a greater degree of co-operation within family groups than side-striped jackals, which occur where water is more plentiful.

The abundance of termites, ants and other insects in the area has resulted in the evolution of some wonderful specialists such as bat-eared foxes, aardvarks and aardwolves. Although they look quite different, they have common characteristics such as weak teeth and jaws, a large sticky tongue and acute powers of hearing.

The aardvark is an extraordinary looking creature, resembling a fat pig with a long snout. A solitary and nocturnal feeder, it can cover more than 30 kilometres nightly in search of insect prey. The aardvark's special adaptations

Trees are a lifeline in the sands of the Kalahari. A shepherd's tree in the ochre dunes of the south stabilises the sands and provides food and cover for many creatures.

In the cool of the night the Kalahari comes alive. A bushbaby (opposite) and tree rat (this page, bottom left) remain in the relative safety of thorny acacia trees. A white-faced owl (top) with its sharp night vision perches nearby. A bat-eared fox (bottom right) can detect insect movements with its large ears.

28

Social ground squirrels (top) live in communal burrows. They keep cool in the day by sand bathing and using their fluffy tails as a shade parasol against the blazing sun. The harvester termite (bottom left), which feeds off grass, is eaten by many creatures, including the spider (bottom right).

The spiny agama (top left) and sand lizard (top right) obtain moisture by feeding on harvester termites. The burrowing frog (middle) survives by remaining underground until it rains. The juvenile sand lizard (bottom right) warns off potential predators by mimicking the distasteful Anthia beetle (bottom left).

The salty crust of the pans (below) was formed when Lake Makgadikgadi's water dried up, creating the largest salt pans in the world (opposite top). After rain the pans are covered by shallow sheets of water (opposite bottom), which attract thousands of birds and animals.

Following well-used trails, herds of animals such as zebras (this page, top) congregate to drink at small, rain-filled pans. Lions (bottom) follow in their wake. The wet-season availability of water and food gives a lion cub (opposite) a better chance of survival.

All the Kalahari's animals will drink if water is available – even the desert unicorn, the gemsbok (below), which can survive without drinking if necessary. Giraffes (opposite) have special valves in the blood vessels of their necks so that blood does not rush to the brain when they bend down to drink.

Transformed by rain, the Kalahari grasslands (opposite) are flushed green and studded with colourful flowers. Leopard tortoises (this page, top) emerge from their dry-season retreats, stimulated by the rain to mate. Their protective shell saves them from inquisitive lions (bottom).

The palm belt, stretching north of Ntwetwe Pan, consists of Hyphaene *palms, which grow in shallow water and were perhaps first brought here by elephants. The palms provide nest sites for birds, and give shade to animals in the open vastness of the pans.*

include a long fleshy nose which is very sensitive to smell. Inside the nostrils are numerous fine hairs, which help to keep out dust and sand as the creature sniffs for insects. The sensitive snout hairs help to detect the movement of insects underground. The aardvark's thick spade-like claws can break open rock-hard termite mounds from which it laps up termites with its long sticky tongue. Less well-equipped termite eaters such as aardwolves and bat-eared foxes often follow aardvarks as they forage.

Aardvarks visit several termite mounds in their territories at regular intervals, returning before the termites' repairs on the broken side of their clay mounds harden fully. The powerful claws affect the animal's gait, which is slow and lumbering, making it easy prey for larger predators. Aardvarks dig different types of burrows: shallow feeding scrapes in the earth or sides of termite mounds; temporary burrows, or bolt-holes, with one chamber; and permanent burrows with many chambers where a female raises her young.

When chased, an aardvark will make a dash for a bolt-hole or, if it cannot reach one, digs to create another at fantastic speed. Disused aardvark burrows are popular with creatures that do not have such powerful claws for digging but can modify an existing burrow for their needs. In the Kalahari, 17 mammal, 1 bird and 2 reptile species have been recorded using aardvark burrows.

Bat-eared foxes are more sociable than silver foxes and less nocturnal than aardvarks. They hunt at night, but spend much time outside their burrows in the day, lying in the sun, playing and grooming. Small and delicately built, they have slim legs and sharp muzzles that offset huge parabolic ears, used for locating termite prey.

Bat-eared foxes are almost defenceless and are preyed on by carnivores such as brown hyaenas, as well as martial eagles and other large birds of prey. The only large carnivore against which the bat-eared fox has any chance is probably the black-backed jackal. If a jackal comes near, an alert fox will arch its back and tail in an alarm signal to others. These foxes 'stot' in the same way as springboks, and may mob the irritated jackal while keeping it in constant view. If a jackal approaches a den with cubs, the parents are alerted by high-pitched mobbing barks and any foxes nearby rush to the den to assist in defending the young.

Bat-eared foxes pair for life. They live in communal burrows but forage alone to avoid distraction or competition when searching for their scattered insect prey. Individuals out foraging maintain contact with each other with soft whistling calls and hold their bushy black-tipped tails erect on the appearance of a predator as a rallying signal to others. They cover their feeding areas rapidly, zig-zagging from one spot to another, stopping to put an ear to the ground to listen for subterranean insect activity.

These foxes eat mainly harvester termites, but will also dig up larvae of tenebrionid beetles and scorpions, sometimes severing the poisonous tail before consuming the scorpion. Seasonal change in termite activity dictates when the foxes are out foraging. When harvester termites are active during the day in winter, so too are bat-eared foxes. They are more flexible feeders than aardvarks, who prefer to change their diet to ants in the cold dry season rather than change their nocturnal habits.

Crude calculations show that insect-eating creatures consume billions of insects per square kilometre per year and are important in maintaining a balance in delicate arid ecosystems. Harvester termites themselves have a major effect on the availability of grass since they can remove up to half the annual grass harvest. In times of drought they are capable of removing the entire grass cover, especially on lands where the larger termite predators have been exterminated. It is ironic that for centuries farmers have killed foxes and aardwolves as vermin when these insect-eaters play an important role in conserving grasslands by controlling the numbers of harvester termites.

The desert hyaena

No carnivore has desert adaptations to rival those of the brown hyaena. This hyaena has long brown fur with a tawny-white mantle of longer hair on the shoulders. Such a coat – unexpected in the hot habitat in which the brown hyaena occurs – is necessary in the cold of desert nights, particularly in winter when temperatures drop below freezing point.

Brown hyaenas have heavy shoulders and powerful jaws typical of the hyaena family, but they are no competition for the more powerful spotted hyaena. Brown hyaenas feed mainly on the kills of other carnivores and use their broad muzzles and strong jaws to break open bones, which, together with dry skin, are generally the only remains of a kill. These shy creatures forage alone at night, relying on their large upstanding ears to pick up the slightest sounds, yet as scavengers they are courageous and steal from large predators. They observe the movements of leopards and lions, and also locate kills by watching for wheeling vultures or listening for the cries of jackals.

Relations between the large predators of the Kalahari are never friendly, even if there is no kill to fight over. Every predator is prey to another, and although size and strength are advantages, the young of all are vulnerable. Small carnivores such as jackals and bat-eared foxes are preyed on by all the large predators, and brown hyaenas are often killed by lions – the 'king' for whom they are no match. Leopards and cheetahs, surprisingly, immediately relinquish a kill to brown hyaenas for these more delicate felines can suffer severe injury from the hyaena's powerful jaws. In the dry season, when lions have left their normal territories, brown hyaenas are top of the scavenging hierarchy.

The social behaviour of brown hyaenas is much more complex than was thought. Their lonely wanderings for food are an adaptation to a harsh place, where food is scarce and widely scattered. Yet they are social creatures, marking grass stems and twigs with a paste from special rectal pouches, which acts as chemical communication to others in the area. Each individual's scent is a 'calling card' telling others of its identity, social rank and time of passing. The 10 or so individuals that share a common range are members of the same 'clan'. When their paths cross on feeding trips there is an elaborate ritual of greeting, and a strong hierarchy of dominance exists among them.

The range of a typical brown hyaena clan covers about 200 square kilometres, larger in times of drought. Each territory includes an area of fossil river valley, where there is a short-lived abundance of kills from lions, leopards and cheetahs to feed on in the wet season. In the dry season the clan enlarges its range to the woodlands and thornscrub of the dunes and plains, in keeping with the movements of antelopes and lions. They also search for tubers, fruits and smaller prey such as rodents, birds, termites and insects. This varied menu supplies their only moisture for many months. When hyaenas find a kill they usually hide or 'cache' some food – particularly when unexpected abundance such as a nest of ostrich eggs is discovered. Few carnivores show this kind of behavioural adaptation to life in an arid wilderness.

A female brown hyaena gives birth in the den, producing a brood of one to four cubs. In the first months she forages alone, but returns to the cubs about twice a night to suckle them. When the cubs are three or four months old, the mother picks them up one by one and carries them to a a communal 'nursery den' within the territory, which is home to other cubs and females of her clan. The young cubs spend the rest of their childhood here, living with other youngsters. All the cubs are generally related since females remain in the clan into which they are born; only males disperse. Only one female usually gives birth each year, which puts a limit on the number of young in the communal den.

Every female hyaena in the clan brings some food to the den when she can, even if she has had no young that year. Some males also bring food to the nursery, and a nursing female will feed other cubs as well as her own. The group thus co-operates to feed the youngsters, which is more effective than the efforts of a lone mother who cannot leave her young for long. The communal den is a remarkable adaptation to life in the harshness of the central Kalahari.

When alone, the cubs are constantly alert for the sound of an approaching predator, diving when alarmed for the safety of the den. Inside the large underground chamber are many small bolt-holes dug by the cubs themselves. Here they are quite safe from marauding lions and leopards. The young remain in the den until they are about 18 months old, when they leave for the first time under the guidance of an adult. After a few months they have enough experience of their range to begin foraging alone.

Nocturnal cats

The black-foot inhabits the arid grasslands of the Kalahari – a spitfire of a cat, hissing and snarling at potential danger with green-gold eyes flashing, teeth bared and ears flat against a rounded head. These cats are late risers, emerging to hunt several hours after sunset. Little is known about these secretive and nocturnal felines. They are the smallest of the African wild cats, weighing just over one kilogram. During the day, they usually take refuge in the hollow of a termite mound – hence the nickname 'anthill tiger'.

Lions are generally nocturnal hunters but never more strongly so than in the Kalahari. There is a definite survival advantage to hunting in the cool of night, when water loss is minimised. Lions are the only distinctly social members of the cat family, living and hunting in prides. In arid habitats, however, the pride structure breaks down in the dry season. Although adult lions have adapted their social behaviour to cope with the dryness of the Kalahari, conditions are hard for cubs. Juvenile mortality is very high among lions. Sometimes a hungry lioness has to abandon her cubs for several days while she hunts, and she may return to find that they have been killed by another predator or even that they have died of thirst or starvation.

Lions hunt giraffes, kudus and gemsboks in the dune woodlands and the valleys, but turn to much smaller prey, such as rodents, porcupines, birds and springhares, with the onset of summer when their larger prey begin increasingly to scatter. In the Kalahari, 50 per cent of all lion kills are of small creatures, compared to only one per cent among Serengeti lions.

In the dry season, or in times of drought, the lion pride disintegrates. Its range may expand some 500 per cent, from a few hundred to several thousand square kilometres. Individuals wander alone much more and female lions may be alone with their cubs for many months, mixing with any strange lions they might happen to meet, changing prides and pride areas frequently and mating with strange males or nursing strange cubs.

In the depths of the dry season dawn brings another day of scorching heat and no rain. The pans are dry and the grasslands are empty except for the desert specialists – gemsboks and springboks – and those unusual termite eaters, aardvarks and aardwolves, and night creatures such as brown hyaenas and black-backed jackals. Resilient and well adapted, they remain in the Kalahari and eke out a precarious existence in an unforgiving land.

CHAPTER THREE

Makgadikgadi Pans

the sun beats down on the baked surface of a huge dry lake bed. All around is a snow-like whiteness that blinds and dazzles. There is no horizon; somewhere the land meets the pale cloudless sky and mirages give the impression of water. There is no sense of time or place. It is like being in a huge and hot vacuum.

The wind announces the end of the day, with no barrier to slow it down. It screams along the hot ground, occasionally losing control and spiralling upwards in a twisting tornado. The sun sinks slowly, a fireball that colours the land orange, while on the other side of the sky the full moon rises. When darkness falls the landscape is once again transformed. Moonlight bathes the ground in a silver light that picks out the faint rise and fall of low, crescent-shaped dunes. The horizon is clear now. Perfectly straight, it cuts this mystical world in half. The star-studded sky forms the upper part of the sphere, the silver-white land the lower. The only sound is the wind.

This is Makgadikgadi, a vast and ancient inland drainage basin of the Kalahari composed chiefly of two major pans – Ntwetwe and Sua. Geologists have discovered prehistoric shorelines that marked the fluctuating perimeter of a huge fossil lake. This enormous depression was once the site of one of the largest lakes ever in Africa. The crusty white surface is composed of saline deposits left behind as the lake's waters were burnt off by the sun. Covering an area of 37 000 square kilometres, Makgadikgadi is the largest area of salt pans in the world. What are the secrets of this harsh white land? Where did the water come from, and where did it all go? Although man has at last begun to unearth the story of their origin, the Makgadikgadi pans remain a mystery.

The drying of the Kalahari reached a climax some three million years ago and was followed by a period of much higher rainfall. As the climate became wetter, great rivers – Okavango, Chobe and Zambezi – flowed once more,

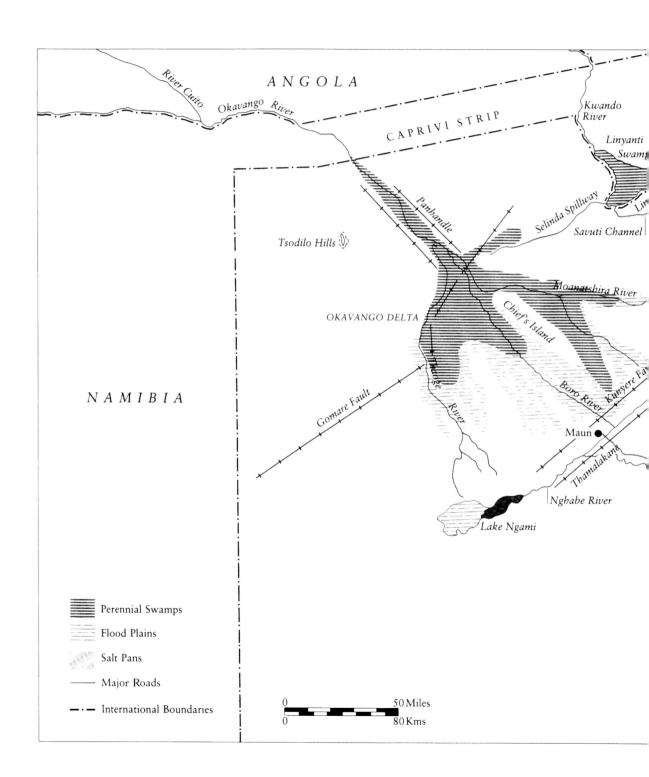

ANGOLA

River Cuito

Okavango River

CAPRIVI STRIP

Kwando River

Linyanti Swamp

Panhandle

Selinda Spillway

Savuti Channel

Tsodilo Hills

Moanatshira River

OKAVANGO DELTA

Chief's Island

Boro River

Kunyere Fault

NAMIBIA

Gomare Fault

Thaoge River

Maun

Thamalakane

Nghabe River

Lake Ngami

Perennial Swamps

Flood Plains

Salt Pans

Major Roads

International Boundaries

0   50 Miles
0   80 Kms

running south-eastwards via the Limpopo into the Indian Ocean. About two million years ago an up-warping of the earth's crust created a fault, the Kalahari-Zimbabwe Axis, which interrupted the flow of these huge rivers, causing them to pond back and gradually fill the immense basin of Makgadikgadi.

An ancient lake

The size of the resulting lake fluctuated with the climatic conditions prevailing at the time. To an experienced eye the different shorelines can still be seen around the perimeters of the pans. It is hard to believe that in this harsh and waterless place there was once a lake with deep fresh waters teeming with fish, birds and crocodiles – a place where early man fished and hunted.

At its maximum size (around 60 000 square kilometres), Lake Makgadikgadi included large areas of what is now the Okavango Delta. The lake would have had an hour-glass shape, with the Okavango depression as one part and the larger Makgadikgadi depression the other, connected by a narrow waist through which the Boteti river valley runs. Some 20 000 years ago, the drainage basin was probably full to capacity so the waters spilled northwards, flowing into the Middle Zambezi.

From here the waters pushed eastwards to the ocean, forming the Victoria Falls in the process and linking the Upper and Middle Zambezi into one large river. Lake Makgadikgadi was no doubt partly drained by the seaward

release of this large quantity of water, but other factors were involved in its gradual desiccation. The climate became hotter, causing rivers to carry less water and the lake to shrink from evaporation. By 10 000 years ago the drying of the Kalahari was well under way. Sediments carried by the Okavango River were increasingly deposited in Lake Okavango, together with wind-blown sands from the shrinking shorelines of the lakes. Eventually the sands and sediments formed the raised cone-shaped fan – actually a large alluvial fan – that characterises the Delta.

The formation of a series of faults, including the Thamalakane Fault, isolated the Okavango from the Makgadikgadi depression. This helped to reduce the amount of water flowing into the lake. As Lake Makgadikgadi continued to shrink the area must have become a series of smaller lakes, which fluctuated in size and eventually disappeared. In addition to the two biggest pans, Ntwetwe and Sua, there are many smaller ones: Nxai, Kudiakau and the drying remnants of the recent lakes – Ngami, Mababe and Xau. Of the water, all that remains is the Okavango Delta. As the great lake slowly shrank, grasslands formed on its edges and salts became increasingly concentrated as the lake fragments shrank through evaporation. Finally the sun burned off the last of the water, leaving behind a brittle crust of white salts at the lowest points.

In the dazzling heat and burning alkalinity of the salt pans, nothing grows. Here and there a crescent-shaped island of sand, sculpted by wind

Baobabs occur in scattered groups around the edges of the Makgadikgadi pans; their swollen trunks hold great quantities of water, enabling them to survive long periods of drought. Hollows in the trunks provide safe nest sites for birds such as barn owls.

The martial eagle (below) and its mate raise their young high up in a massive nest in mopane woodlands, which are an important habitat since their pans (opposite top) retain water long into the dry season. The mopane moth caterpillar (opposite bottom) feeds on the leaves of mopane trees.

An elephant (opposite) roams the northern woodlands after rain, using mopane pans as watering points on its journey. An animal that has died amongst the trees is soon detected by vultures (this page, top). Mopane squirrels (bottom) live in family groups in tree hollows.

Relations between carnivores are never friendly, particularly at a kill. Vultures wait impatiently while spotted hyaenas feed (opposite top). Lions (below and opposite bottom) and spotted hyaenas are almost equal in the feeding hierarchy – the outcome usually depends on strength of numbers.

Zebras (below) migrate to the Makgadikgadi pans after rain but, like wildebeests (opposite bottom), they remain in the area only as long as water is available. The springhare (opposite top), a large rodent, is a resident species which is able to survive on moisture from its food.

Elephants sometimes damage the trees they feed on; however, they also assist in the dispersal and germination of new trees. After eating acacia pods, elephants pass out intact the seeds intact (this page, top), which germinate (bottom) in moist and nutrient-rich conditions.

Drying pans act as a signal perhaps for nomadic buffaloes to return to the permanent rivers and swamps before the interior dries up completely.
OVERLEAF: *Zebras at sunset.*

and the water currents of the former lake, rises high enough above the salts to permit the growth of spiky grass and the occasional stunted acacia. Such areas penetrate the pans in long ridges and islets that support some vegetation.

Burrowing specialists

Although criss-crossing tracks can be seen meandering across the pans as creatures move from one grass-covered island to another, no animals live on the pans. A specialised lizard, the Makgadikgadi spiny agama, survives under the salt bushes on the edges. It feeds on tenebrionid beetles and harvester termites, climbing up on grass clumps to cool in the wind and burying itself in the sand to hide from predators.

Few animals can survive in the area throughout the year. During the dry season the pans are entirely waterless. The salt crust of the ancient lake bed cracks as the mud beneath shrinks, and around its edges the grasses are baked a brittle brown. Those animals that can remain in the area have specialised feeding strategies to obtain water.

Springboks are resident in the palm grasslands fringing the pans, preferring the open habitat where they can detect predators from afar. They obtain moisture by feeding on succulent plants, browsing on bushes and digging for underground tubers. Cheetahs are their main predators, and vast open stretches of grassland offer perfect hunting grounds for these magnificent sprinters. Like other predators, cheetahs obtain moisture from the blood of their prey. They also hunt at night to catch their second most abundant prey, springhares.

The springhare is a large nocturnal rodent unique to Africa. With its shaggy ginger coat, long and powerful hind legs, large ears and bushy tail, it looks like a mixture of a rabbit and a small kangaroo. The dry Kalahari grasslands seem an unlikely place for such a creature. Springhares are prolific diggers, living in burrows excavated from the soft sands and emerging at night to feed, dashing back to their burrows when alarmed. They prefer the short grasses that grow on the very edges of the salt pans, for these are higher in minerals and protein and are not too tall, making predator detection easier.

Springhares hop on their kangaroo-like hind legs, using the short front legs to feed as they pluck and eat the succulent grass bases. On moonlit nights the shadows of palm trees provide them with a certain amount of cover. Like many nocturnal creatures springhares are not highly social, but feed in groups for safety. These tasty rodents are an important food source for carnivores, including man. Disused springhare burrows are taken over by bat-eared foxes, silver foxes, mongooses and even snakes.

There are other burrows scattered among the sandy grasslands, since remaining underground is the best strategy to avoid the intense heat of summer, when temperatures in the open rise to over 60°C. Small openings in the sand are evidence of the homes of scorpions, which are better able to withstand high temperatures than almost any other creature. The disused burrows of rodents, bat-eared foxes and aardvarks provide humid retreats for insects, snakes and lizards. Each burrow has a fascinating sequence of ownership as one species leaves and another takes over.

Aardwolves are mysterious creatures, seldom seen even though they are quite abundant around the Makgadikgadi pans. The common name of this slender hyaena, which lives much of its life underground, comes from Afrikaans, meaning 'earth wolf'. The aardwolf's high shoulders and sloping back are typically hyaenid, but it is a quarter of the size and weight of the brown hyaena. A highly specialised animal, it lives exclusively on insects, having evolved dentition so weak that its poorly-developed cheek teeth are unable to capture or chew a more fleshy meal.

Aardwolves are particularly vulnerable to large predators like lions, leopards and hyaenas. Burrows are important for their safety and, although they use the abandoned burrows of springhares and aardvarks, they also dig their own dens, especially in the softer sands around the edges of the pans. Some dens are for resting in during the day or raising the young; deeper burrows scattered throughout the range are boltholes in which to escape.

The aardwolf's sense of hearing is highly developed. Large ears, similar in shape and size to those of the bat-eared fox, help this nocturnal creature to detect and locate insect prey,

which it then laps up with a broad and sticky tongue. In winter when harvester termites forage during the day the aardwolf switches its attention to snouted termites, which continue to be active at night.

The sense of smell also plays a major role in the everyday life of the shy and solitary aardwolf. It is a prolific scent marker and, like other hyaenas, is equipped with anal scent glands with which to mark or 'paste' an object with a musky secretion. Aardwolves have different types of marking behaviour. Important areas such as the den in their territory or range are marked with several large blobs of secretion on a grass stem. A minute amount is also left on a grass stem in the area in which they are feeding, perhaps to indicate that the area has already been visited.

Ostriches occasionally wander across the pans – huge birds dwarfed in the emptiness. Able to withstand intense heat and to live with hardly any water, essential requirements for survival here, this flightless bird has nasal glands through which it excretes excess salts from its body with no wasteful loss of water. To protect its body from the heat that beats down from the sun and is radiated up from the white surface of the salt pans, it fluffs up its back feathers and fans itself with its large wings, sometimes drooping them loosely at their sides.

The ostrich is the largest bird on earth. Flightless, its success is remarkable in a land full of dangerous predators. Birds such as the dodo in Mauritius and the kiwi in New Zealand lost the power of flight presumably because there was no danger from predators – until the arrival of man and the domestic cat, which hunted young chicks. This sudden influx of predators resulted in the extinction of the dodo and the endangering of the kiwi. In Africa, where the list of large predators is formidable, one wonders why the ostrich lost its ability to fly.

Fossil finds show that ostriches probably evolved in Europe some 50 million years ago. Already flightless, the birds migrated southwards, perhaps pushed by the advancing Ice Age, walking some 10 000 kilometres until they reached the southernmost part of their natural range in southern Africa. The size of the bird, probably the reason it cannot fly, is a clue to its great success on the African continent. Immensely strong legs enable it to outrun most predators while sharp claws and a powerful kick allow an adult bird to protect itself from even a lion attack.

Ostriches have evolved an elaborate social organisation, which presumably contributes to the survival of chicks. Adult birds nest communally, several females laying their eggs in one nest, which is incubated by only a territorial male and his hen. The conspicuous black and white plumage of the males makes them more vulnerable to predators, resulting in more females than males in a population. In addition, the ostrich egg is smaller in relation to the adult bird's size than the eggs of most other birds. Although a female may lay only six or seven eggs, she can incubate three times that number.

It therefore makes sense for the 'major' hen to incubate the eggs of females that do not have their own mate and nest.

The male and the major hen (the male at night and the female by day) do benefit from incubating, for six dangerous weeks, a clutch of eggs, half of which belong to other females. We know that the major female can recognise her own eggs, which she pushes to the centre of the nest. Since the eggs of the minor hens are more likely to be taken first by predators, this enhances the chances of her own eggs surviving by 'dilution'. Ostrich eggs are preyed on by brown hyaenas and Egyptian vultures, among others.

The pair also take care of all the chicks, forming huge 'crèches' as they adopt young birds from nearby nesting pairs. Crèches of over a hundred young ostriches have been seen at Makgadikgadi. Again this behaviour increases the chances of survival by 'diluting' the effects of predation.

The palm belt

The palm belt that sweeps around the northwest of Ntwetwe Pan is a spectacularly beautiful anomaly in the short grasslands of this arid wilderness. Palm groves stretch to the white sands and salts on the fringes of pans, the rustle and stirring of their fan-shaped fronds evocative of the sound of waves on the sandy shore of the lake that once was.

Hyphaene palms grow well in areas with a slightly saline water-table, which few other trees can tolerate. Their large ginger-coloured fruits are eaten by many creatures, but only elephants are large enough to disperse their seeds over a long distance. Today few elephants range as far as the Makgadikgadi pans since the supply of fresh water is unreliable. The groves of palms suggest that they were once here in large numbers and may have brought in their stomachs the seeds of palms from the Okavango Delta and the great rivers of the north.

Palms stand as the only elevation in the grasslands, providing roosting and nesting sites for birds in the region. Vultures nest on the very tops of palm trees, in large constructions made of sticks and twigs. Often they are associated with red-necked falcons, which nest lower down and lay their eggs in the hollow formed where a frond joins the slender grey stem of the palm.

Most of this falcon's prey is caught on the wing and no doubt includes other residents of the palm tree's crown, such as bats and the slender long-winged palm swift. The latter are specialised inhabitants of *Hyphaene* palms and roost beneath the fronds at night, clinging to the underside, rocked by the wind. They build a cup-shaped nest of saliva, feathers and mud, glued to the midrib, the blade of the frond drawn around as camouflage.

Acacia woodlands

Beyond the palm belt the Makgadikgadi grasslands merge into acacia woodlands of spiky blackthorn acacias dotted with small islands of taller acacias which provide shade in the heat.

Despite its inhospitable appearance, the acacia is a valuable food source for browsing animals such as kudus and giraffes and a dry-season alternative to grasses for springboks and gemsboks. Acacia leaves are higher in protein than most other leaves and the tree has leaves even in the driest of times, replacing them as soon as they die. The seed pods and flowers are an added bonus, with twice the protein content of even the most nutritious grasses.

Secretary birds find good nesting sites in the bushy thickets of acacia when they breed in summer. The adult birds stalk through the long grass, black head-quills shaking with each stride of their long legs. Eagle-sharp eyes and a powerful curved beak are a deadly combination for catching poisonous snakes such as the slow-moving but quick-striking and deadly puff adder. The secretary bird repeatedly bats the striking snake with the leading edges of its wings until the snake is exhausted and then moves in for the kill – a few slashes with its lethal claws. Although renowned hunters of large snakes, secretary birds usually seek smaller prey when feeding their chicks.

Both male and female secretary birds care for the chicks, returning alternately to feed them after foraging in the grasslands. Food is stored in the crop and regurgitated to the begging chicks. The parents also carry water in their crop since the thirsty chicks are exposed to relentless heat in the shadeless nest. On visits the parents bring nesting material to re-line and maintain the large nest. When nearly fledged the chicks begin exercising themselves by standing on the nest and flapping their wings.

Silent giants

A cluster of baobabs on the arid edges of the pans dwarf the acacias and palms. Baobabs live to a great age and some may be over 3 000 years old – offspring of trees that stood on the edge of the great Lake Makgadikgadi. Each swollen trunk may hold up to 9 000 litres of water, enabling the tree to survive long periods of drought. The extraordinary baobabs are a world of their own, providing food, cover and water in a harsh environment. The old trees have hollows carved long ago by people who sought refuge inside the mighty trunks or extracted water from the fibrous wood-pulp. There is always life in these hollows.

At dusk the ghostly white form of a barn owl perches at the entrance to a baobab hollow. With a screeching call it sets off, gliding over the grasslands beyond the baobab grove and the empty salt pan. The male owl is out hunting for food to feed his mate who broods their eggs. Rodents living in colonies in burrows in the grass nearby are his favourite prey. When they are scarce, he hunts bats, scorpions, skinks and lizards – the winter diet of this arid land.

In the huge hollow of the baobab there is often more than one breeding pair of adult barn owls, which use the same roost and nest sites year after year. The bond between a pair is strong and they will probably spend most of the year roosting together even when their young have flown the nest.

The eggs hatch after a month, but the chicks are undeveloped and without feathers, huddling together for warmth and physical support in the first weeks. It is only in their eighth week that the young barn owls first leave the nest. They remain near the baobab hollow – one of the safest places in the stark exposed habitat of the pan.

The rains

Although a waving blanket of golden stems still covers the grasslands, grazing animals begin to disperse in search of more succulent vegetation and water-dependent animals migrate to areas of permanent water. This pattern of animal mobility gives the grasses a rest season that enables remarkable growth in the harsh and difficult Kalahari habitat. If the fragile balance were disturbed and the grasses over-grazed and uprooted, the sands would be let loose on their crazy wanderings, driven by the wind.

After a long year with no water, the build-up to rain is dramatic. The first sign is an intense and heavy heat. There is a deathly quiet and no movement. Most animals are in their burrows or resting in whatever shade they can find. Heat waves distort the air and mirages give the impression of water shimmering over the ancient lake bed. Winds pick up with a sudden violence. Whirlwinds and dust devils rise into the blackening sky, carrying hot air and dust as they lean forwards crazily and speed across the pans. Rainstorms fall locally, filling shallow pans with water and attracting large herds of springboks to the new flush of green grass.

Rain that falls throughout this immense area gradually drains towards the Makgadikgadi pans. Rivulets run into narrow channels, flowing into sandy stream beds. Dry river beds are briefly flushed with water and small pans fill up. Although the rainstorms are scattered and brief, the Makgadikgadi basin soon fills with a sheet of shallow water that stretches to the horizon.

The pans are transformed by the simple event of rain. Scattered in the emerald carpet of newly-sprouted grasses are the colourful flowers of mesembryanthemums, aloes, melons and other desert succulents which complete their lifecycle quickly, before dryness arrives again. Leopard tortoises, which have been in semi-hibernation during the dry hot months before the rains, emerge from their retreats beneath logs and under soil.

The arrival of the rains stimulates animals to mate. In a very vocal affair the male tortoise pushes his mate, who is much larger than he is, for hours or even days until she is in a suitable position. She lays her eggs in the ground, young soft-shelled tortoises emerging the following year with the rains. The hard shell of the adults makes them difficult to kill although lions will play with one for hours. Young tortoises, however, are preyed on by many carnivores. Eagles drop them from the air to break open the soft shell.

In the saline waters of smaller pans there is an unexpected burst of life. Salty depressions abound with frogs and tadpoles, which feed on aquatic insects which, in turn, are hunted by small terrapins, semi-aquatic relatives of the tortoise. Helmeted terrapins remain buried deep beneath the sand for months, maybe even years. Having spent the dry period in aestivation, they emerge as soon as the pans hold water. They can often be seen basking in the sun, but are most at home in the water, where they wait in ambush for a passing tadpole or frog that has also emerged with the wet.

The female helmeted terrapin digs into earth away from the water in order to lay her eggs in a shallow chamber. Since the sunbaked ground is extraordinarily hard, she softens the spot with her body water. Large and relatively powerful claws provide useful service since digging into hard earth is important to the survival of these animals. As the pans dry out the adult terrapins bury themselves deep into the earth again until the next rain.

The sudden availability of water opens the grasslands to zebras and wildebeests, who abandon their retreats of permanent water and follow the rains. They arrive at Makgadikgadi in thousands. Scattered throughout the palm belt, they feed on the new grasses near the salt pans. The grasses are higher in mineral content and relatively abundant as scattered groups of springboks are the only large herbivores that have been feeding on them.

Because of the large number of animals grouped together, social organisation among migratory wildebeests is minimal. Males remain in the vicinity of females, forming temporary territories. A termite mound is often a central focus for male wildebeests attempting to collect potential mates. Their low grunting as they call to passing groups of females becomes a chorus-like mantra when hundreds of animals are on the move. Males fight frequently, fiercely clashing horns and sparring on their knees. In a comic form of territorial behaviour known as 'cavorting' they leap and bound in displays to one another, and can become so absorbed in this that they are easily preyed on by lions that follow the seasonal migration.

The wildebeests that arrive at the pans during the rains calve in remarkable synchrony, probably not as close though as in the Serengeti in Tanzania, where 80 per cent of wildebeest calves are born within three weeks. As in ostrich crèches, this abundance of young has the effect of 'diluting' predation for there are only so many predators in one place at one time.

The arrival of so many grazing animals and their predators transforms the grasslands. However, daytime temperatures are still high, and most animals feed only in the early morning, evening and at night. Nomadic lions wait for the cool of darkness before they set out to hunt. In the stillness of the noonday heat the only sound is the shrill call of the red-crested korhaan parachuting out of the sky in a bizarre mating display.

As the sun slides to the west the wind picks up and begins to cool the scorching day. Herds of wildebeests, zebras and springboks stir from their resting places beneath the palm groves. As they trek across the grasslands the wind whips up the sand kicked loose by their hooves; the landscape filled with regiments of dark, moving shapes dwarfed by lines of palms that mark the boundary between earth and sky. A pool of water sparkles unexpectedly in the dusty plains. It is towards this that the lines of animals are slowly moving.

There is an air of nervous excitement as the herds walk towards the water, no doubt aware of their vulnerability to predators as they drop their guard and lower their heads to drink. Wildebeests lead the advancing lines of animals while zebra stallions canter around the periphery, controlling their harems with high-pitched barking calls. The wildebeests at the head of the line might nervously turn back, and so might the next few, until at last one wades belly-deep into the water to drink. After this first brave move there is a surge of animals towards the waterhole. The zebras still hold back for a few minutes, nervously searching for predators with their acute sense of smell, sight and hearing.

The Nata delta

A dramatic event occurs with the arrival of the rains in the Sua pan in the north-eastern section of Makgadikgadi. The Nata River, which rises in the highlands of Zimbabwe, flows only when there is rain. It empties its waters into the Sua pan, forming a second but (compared with Okavango) much smaller inland delta in the Kalahari. Soon the dry lake bed is covered by a shallow sheet of water that stretches for several hundred square kilometres, reflecting the powder-blue of the sky. The waters become saline as the crusty salts on the pan's surface dissolve and are concentrated by evaporation. Despite this salinity, the arrival of water brings life. As if by a miracle the warm shallows become alive with millions of tiny shrimps hatched from eggs buried in the white salt mud. Algae also flourish in the saline water.

The eggs of the brine shrimp are one of the most resilient forms of life on earth. They are superbly adapted to the harsh and unstable environment of the Kalahari salt pans, surviving in the salt mud under great extremes of temperature, totally desiccated and almost inert. Tests on such eggs have failed to detect a metabolism of one ten-thousandth of normal levels – to all intents and purposes they are dead. They can remain in this form for many years, but as soon as the salt pans flood they hatch into delicate white shrimps that swim upside down propelled by feathery limbs. Millions of tonnes of brine shrimps hatch out with the flooding of the Sua pan, constituting the base of a massive food chain.

Birds respond quickly to this abundance of food. Greater and lesser flamingoes arrive in thousands, sometimes even tens of thousands.

Winged migrants, they come, perhaps, from other large pans in southern Africa, such as Etosha, or the soda lakes of the Great Rift Valley, a journey of several thousand kilometres. Flamingoes use their inverted beak as a pump to filter and extract their food from the salty waters. The delta of the Sua pan is the largest recorded breeding area for greater flamingoes in all of Africa.

Wading birds and ducks – avocets, Hottentot and red-billed teals, dabchicks, blacksmith plovers and black-winged stilts – forage along the muddy edges of fresh water near the river mouth, picking for the new aquatic life the Nata River has brought down. This is a good time for birds to have their young, and exposed nests of ground-nesting birds are scattered along the edges of the pan. Their eggs provide food for the common egg-eater snake, which has no fangs and no venom, living exclusively on eggs. The egg-eater's head is small, and it must dislocate its jaws in order to swallow an egg. Several dozen bony projections in its throat puncture the eggshell to release its contents and the emptied shell is regurgitated in a neat package.

At dusk flocks of white pelicans return from their feeding grounds on the river and further away. Leaving the thermals, they wheel in the sky and settle like aircraft carriers on the glassy water. The sun slides over the horizon tinging the water sky-pink to match the pink flamingoes that have settled for the night in this extraordinary and timeless world.

CHAPTER FOUR

Nomads

after the brief rains, the relentless heat soon leaves vast tracts of the Kalahari devoid of water. The grasslands and woodlands of the sand plateau and the saline vastness of the Makgadikgadi pans all revert to aridity. Water-dependent animals such as zebras, wildebeests, elephants and buffaloes, which follow the rains into the interior in search of food and minerals, must return to permanent water. In the past the same species probably had a local pattern of movement to obtain water and fresh grazing. As conditions became increasingly arid, the annual treks to water became longer, culminating in journeys today of several hundred kilometres as the animals journey to the Okavango and Chobe wetlands.

Unfortunately, the animal migrations of the Kalahari have not really been understood. Had they been, their sudden and tragic disruption in recent times might not have happened on such a scale. Hundreds of kilometres of fences have been built to control the spread of foot-and-mouth cattle disease and comply with European Union (EU) import regulations. Inadvertently, they carve up and confine large tracts of the Kalahari and block the paths of thousands of wild animals to Okavango water in times of drought. The result has been the loss of more than half the central Kalahari's wildebeest and hartebeest populations. Many traditional migratory routes are now cut off by fences, farms and human habitation. Towards the Chobe, however, the movement of nomadic animals is still largely unhindered, though the patterns of movement are complex and are only now being understood through research.

In the immense sand plateau of the central Kalahari the only permanent waters occur in the Molopo River to the south, the Limpopo to the south-east, and a great water crescent to the north. This northern arc comprises the Okavango Delta, its southern outlets – the Boro and Boteti rivers – and the Chobe with its associated swamplands of Linyanti and the Kwando. These permanent waters provide a refuge for water-dependent animals, enabling a reservoir population to survive until new rains permit them to venture once more into the interior.

Although these nomads respond to the sight, smell and sound of distant storms and rain, much of their migratory behaviour is, no doubt, a traditional response passed on from generation to generation. Elands and hartebeests wander deep into the sand dunes and grasslands of the arid south. Whereas hartebeests dig for tubers in dry periods and are thus able to inhabit the arid sandveldt, elands migrate southwards to the Molopo River and its tributaries in times of drought. They are the largest of Africa's antelopes, roaming the sandveldt in small mixed herds until the need for water or the attraction of local rains brings them together in groups of several thousand as they move southwards. Few such groups are left today.

The wildebeest tragedy

Wildebeests are the most migratory of the Kalahari's animals, occupying and vacating large tracts seemingly at random. They are well adapted to a nomadic life, especially in their breeding behaviour. Whereas most antelope calves have a two-week 'hiding' period in long grass, when they are suckled by the visiting mother, wildebeest calves can stand and travel with the herd within minutes of birth.

Wildebeests are the only large wild herbivores that have to survive the dry season on a grass diet. Occurring in large concentrations and restricted to grass, they are constantly on the move to find grasses sufficiently high in nutrients and water. They move over vast distances, between local patches of rain, but cannot meet their moisture requirements from grass alone during droughts.

As the water pans and grasses dry out, the distant sight and sound of rain beckons the wildebeests. With unerring instinct, heads held low, they begin their plodding march, forming lines and then columns as more and more join the irresistible movement. Their hanging-head posture as they follow in lines may be related to smelling their tracks, since there are glands on the hooves that leave a scent trail. Wildebeests have folded hair-lined nostrils that block out the suffocating dust of thousands of animals on the move.

It was natural for wildebeests to move north to the water crescent formed by the Boteti River and the southern Okavango Delta. However, the erection in 1958 of the Kuke Fence, which stretches 360 kilometres across the northern and central Kalahari, blocked most of this movement. A severe drought that lasted from 1979 to 1983 caused thousands of wildebeests to travel northwards as far as this barricade. Their progress halted, they turned eastwards along the Kuke Fence. Finally, starving and dying of thirst, they reached the fence's end at Lake Xau, which had already been drained by the Orapa diamond mine to feed their reservoir at Mopipi.

As unnaturally large numbers of wildebeests concentrated, the grazing, already depleted by cattle, was quickly exhausted. The result was death for thousands of animals. An estimated 50 000 wildebeests died at Lake Xau in 1983. The fantastic wildebeest migrations of the central Kalahari are now a thing of the past.

In the wet season the wildebeest populations of Makgadikgadi follow a separate and more fixed pattern of movement. They move to the short-grass plains at the palm belt edging the Ntwetwe Pan, to feed on new grasses and to obtain mineral licks. Here most of the females have their calves.

The Boteti River, the outlet of the Delta to which wildebeest herds moved in the dry season, is the river that fed the ancient Lake Makgadikgadi. Now it is largely dry, restricted to a series of pools that are dwarfed by tall and wide banks, the only remnant of its former glory. However, it is still of major importance as the only source of water near Makgadikgadi and the central Kalahari sand plateau − a refuge where animals can survive until the next rains. If the dry season is extended, the grasslands are rapidly depleted and animals must trek over 40 kilometres a day to get from the river pools to good grazing. Many die.

The deep holes dug by Boteti cattle farmers are sometimes the only source of water in the area. Cattle go there to drink by day, but zebras and wildebeests wait for night to fall before venturing out from the security of the Boteti woodlands. The lions that follow the herds from Makgadikgadi are much tempted by the availability of unattended cattle. So severe has been the conflict between cattle farmers and lions that are hunted in retaliation that, according to estimates, there appear to be only 50 lions remaining in Makgadikgadi.

Zebra migrations

The zebra is another water-dependent grazer in Makgadikgadi that migrates, following the rains to areas with lush new grass and returning to permanent water in the dry season. Zebra harems, where one stallion controls a number of mares and his offspring, are well suited to a nomadic lifestyle. There are strong social bonds within harems, reinforced by individuals constantly grooming each other. Each zebra's pattern of stripes is unique and enables individuals in a group to recognise one another easily.

As zebras gather in an area of good grazing, the harem loses its identity and the zebras form concentrations of hundreds of individuals, but as soon as the animals are on the move again the harem re-forms. Bachelor males are constantly looking for females, especially young fillies from other harems, and the fierce fighting seen between stallions is inevitably over the ownership of a female. Zebra mothers are extremely protective of their young, and no other zebra is allowed close to the newborn foal. As they grow older the foals of the harem begin to play together, and other females will protect a foal if the mother is not around.

Zebras once wandered deep into the central Kalahari but became extinct there in the early 1960s, after severe drought in the years after the erection of the Kuke Fence. Zebra migrations still occur north of the Kuke Fence, and several different patterns of movement are currently the subject of research.

The Makgadikgadi zebra population follows a pattern of movement similar to that of wildebeests: during the dry season the zebras move to the Boteti, going to the river to drink in the evening. The hours of darkness are spent in the acacia woodlands on the banks of the river, where they are safer from lions. One animal in a family group remains standing, alert for predators, while the others sleep. They leave the river before dawn to return to their feeding grounds.

Another zebra migration occurs in the north, although at one time this movement may have included that of the Makgadikgadi population. After the rains in November, thousands of zebras congregate on the short grasslands of the Mababe depression and the Savuti Marsh, which was once a lake but dried along with many others. Until recently the Savuti Channel flowed from the northern swamps of Linyanti, but this too has dried up. However, migratory herds still concentrate on the Savuti marshes after rain, attracted by the abundance of short grasses on the open plains. The herds remain on the open grasslands until the start of the dry season in May, at which time zebras leave for areas of permanent water in the northern Linyanti swamps.

The abundance of zebras and antelopes in the Savuti region supports a large and diverse population of predators including lions, leopards, spotted hyaenas and wild dogs. Lions and spotted hyaenas are the most common nocturnal hunters here. Lions in this area have larger prides and smaller territories than the nomadic lions of the Kalahari. Zebras are formidable opponents and the harem's stallion has tremendous spirit, courage and strength. He is constantly on the alert, tirelessly searching out, calling for and returning to his care any lost or lagging members of the harem. As a result, fewer zebra foals are killed than are the young of wildebeests. The strong co-operation among zebras in a harem also leads to asynchronous breeding, unlike that of wildebeests, which are synchronous breeders and calve at the same time.

The spotted hyaena appears to be the dominant carnivore in the area. Despite their scavenging, spotted hyaenas are highly successful hunters, operating in large groups of as many as 20 individuals. Against them even a bull buffalo has little chance. The ability of spotted hyaenas to crush animal bones into fine pieces plays a wide role in the ecology of these areas. White-backed vulture chicks, which are fed on small bone fragments, show calcium-deficiency diseases in those areas where spotted hyaenas have been eradicated.

Individuals among highly social, pack-hunting African wild dogs have learnt a sure way of overpowering their zebra prey. Breeders of horses immobilise a stallion by using a 'nose-twitch' – a piece of leather thong which twists around and grips the upper lip of the animal. Some wild dogs use a similar trick. They will leap up at a fleeing zebra, grasp the striped horse around the lip and bring down the immobilised animal.

Venturing into the interior

Today, with so much of the central Kalahari fenced, the migrations are a ghost of the past. However, north of the Kuke Fence, other animals – elephants and buffaloes the most numerous among them – undergo a seasonal dispersal. They follow a pattern of wet-season dispersal and dry-season concentration at permanent water – a pattern quite different from that of the desert antelopes, gemsboks and springboks, which disperse in the dry season. The dry-season concentration of thousands of elephants along the fringes of permanent water seriously depletes their food supply and so, when the scattered pans are recharged by rain, they move to the interior, travelling to fresh grasses and shrubs that have been rested and renewed.

Elephants and buffaloes once roamed the central Kalahari in the wet season. Its drying in the last decade along with the interference of people and cattle now restricts them to perma-nent waterways such as the Okavango and Chobe and their associated swamps. As soon as the rains come they leave for the woodlands of the interior. Sometimes they venture as far south as the Boteti River and Makgadikgadi, although not all populations are involved in long-distance movement. Within the Delta, a much smaller and more local pattern of dispersal occurs in relation to the rains as well as the annual floods.

The sparse scrub and grass of the sandveldt stretching northwards to the edge of the Delta and the Chobe River give way, with the increase in rainfall, to woodlands. Slight variations in soil type and the rise and dip of thinly masked dunes result in different types of vegetation. Acacia woodlands, with terminalia and lead-wood trees, grow on ridges of deep sand while mopane trees flourish on finer sands and clay soils, dominating vast tracts of the country. From the air, patches, waves and lines of woodlands can be seen to be separated by lagoons and channels of grass. The curving lines of these grass-lands, which look like pools of golden water, indicate areas that were flooded in the past, in wetter times. They occasionally become water-logged after rains, preventing the growth of trees.

The northern woodlands are an important habitat, the mopane woods being the most widespread. Mopanes grow best on soils with poor drainage, occurring in areas of fine sand with a high clay content. They are exceptionally resistant to drought, the tree making internal adjustments to cope with water-related stresses. In ideal conditions mopanes grow tall in dense stands, forming elegant 'cathedral mopane' groves. Where conditions are less ideal they tend to grow as shrubs. The leaves of the mopane are like butterfly wings, each composed of two leaflets, producing a cool dappled shade in the heat of summer. In the intense heat of the noon-day sun the leaflets move closer together to reduce water loss.

The clay soils of mopane woodlands hold water well into the dry season, when the rain-water of sandy regions has long gone. These rain-filled pans sustain elephants, buffaloes and sable and roan antelopes, which wander the woodlands for many months. Wide paths, trodden by elephants over millennia, lead from one water-hole to the next, guiding animals to water as they venture into arid interior. When the pans are almost dry, the nomadic animals gradually make the long trek back to the rivers and swamps, using the pans as staging posts on the journey.

Elephants are constantly enlarging pans by digging for water, cooling their skins with coatings of thick clay mud. As the mud dries, they rub it off their thick hides against nearby trees, which helps remove irritating skin parasites. Some pans originate at the edges of the tall clay mounds of fungus termites, common in mopane woodlands. The mounds are rich in minerals (a by-product of termite saliva and clay soil) and animals come to lick at them, digging at the edges to loosen the salts. Over time a depression forms and collects water, attracting other animals that drink and wallow in the small water-hole. Clay is carried away on their hides, and in this way pans are constantly formed, maintained and deepened.

At the water pan

The woodlands come alive with the arrival of rain. Rivulets of water run down the grey tree trunks, forming channels across the clay sands and draining into the deeper pans. Against a purple sky, laden with rain, crimson mopane leaves burst from their buds, turning into a lime-green flush. The rains attract the large mammals, which leave the rivers and swamps and disperse in small groups. Moving from pan to pan, they are able to penetrate deep into the woodlands of the north, once again.

In the early morning a mixed group of greater kudu, delicate and shy despite their great size, come down to drink. They are joined by flocks of game birds – and the martial eagle. Although these eagles hunt large prey such as duikers and smaller items like mongooses and squirrels, their most abundant prey are helmeted guineafowl, crested francolin and other 'game birds'. The eagles soar at a great height, surveying a woodland territory that may cover as much as 200 square kilometres. If hunting in a limited space like a water pan, the bird parachutes down steeply at speed; on contact it shoots its long legs forward and grasps its prey, killing it on impact.

Buffaloes visit the pans soon after rain. Their massive black shapes emerge menacingly from the trees, curved horns held high, noses sniffing the air for signs of danger. Sable antelopes prefer to drink at midday, cautiously emerging from the shady woods and checking for predators before lowering their heads to drink. The crescent-shaped horns, carried by both males and females, form a battalion of weapons reflected in the water of the pool.

At dusk elephants follow their wide highways to the edge of the water pan, where they cool in the mud and drink their fill before another night of wandering and feeding. They spend time on the sand-dune ridges, relishing the roots of terminalia trees and eating their leaves and seeds. These areas of deep sand contain no water, so their use by elephants is restricted to times when the mopane pans are full, providing a nearby water source. In the twilight thirsty zebras hurry through the woodlands. In the thin rays of evening light branches and trunks form a broken background that camouflages their black and white striped coats. After drinking the zebras are gathered together by the barking calls of stallions and return to the cover of the trees.

At night the mopane woods are a different world, resounding with the noise of crickets. Bats flit over the open surface of pans, catching insects attracted to the warmth that rises from the water. Several species of bats occur in these woodlands, taking different sizes and species of moths and other insects.

On mopane trees

Of the resident woodland animals, mopane tree squirrels are among the liveliest and most charming. They live in groups, sharing the same nest in the hollow of a mopane tree, strangers being immediately chased away.

Social communication is reinforced by smell and touch. The squirrels mark by rubbing their scent glands against each other and spend a great deal of time in mutual grooming. Agile climbers, they scamper from tree to tree and sometimes hang by their feet to reach food on the outermost branches.

Mopane tree squirrels fall prey to many predators – baboons, mongooses, snakes, small cats and birds of prey. When a predator appears, the entire group lines up along a branch, screeching, with tails flicking and heads bobbing. It is an effective mobbing display and sends many an embarrassed predator skulking away. Tree squirrels breed all year round, the male noisily chasing a receptive female before mating. Before her confinement, the female lines the nest hole with leaves and grass.

With the arrival of the rains mopane emperor moths emerge from underground pupae. The mouthparts of the adult moths are undeveloped, so they cannot feed and must mate within a few days of emerging. Females release a pheromone into the air which is picked up by the large feathery antennae of the males. Soon after mating the female mopane moth lays her eggs on the green leaves. Before the eggs hatch, three weeks later, her brief life will have ended.

On hatching, the small green caterpillars must consume their eggshells before they are able to feed on their normal leaf diet. Perhaps a substance in the eggshell allows their digestion to cope with the high content of turpentine-like oils found in green mopane leaves. The caterpillars soon grow fat, black-spotted and large, measuring over six centimetres. Present in vast numbers, they quickly denude a tree of its leaves. The fully grown caterpillars, or 'mopane worms', are a tasty and high-protein food for many, including humans.

Scale insects also lay their eggs on green mopane leaves, their covering of clear sweet gum much sought after by baboons. When the woodlands are still in green leaf, martial eagle pairs begin to rebuild their nests. A pair uses the same nest, which is usually sited in the fork of the largest tree in their territory, for many years. The nest, constructed of sturdy sticks and lined with small twigs, is rebuilt repeatedly, reaching a size of about two metres wide and deep. The female lays a single egg in May, which hatches after an incubation period of 48 days. The male eagle brings food to the female, to feed their chick. When the chick is 10 weeks old it is completely feathered and able to feed itself on food brought to the nest by its parents.

Returning to the wetlands

By the end of the rains many of the larger mammals have ventured far from the wetlands. Elephants, buffaloes, zebras and wildebeests cover great distances as they explore the interior. Some reach as far south as Makgadikgadi, and for a brief time the big game of the north intermingle with the arid-land animals of the south. Less hardy animals such as the sable antelope remain in the mopane woodlands to be closer to permanent water.

Herds of female sables and their young cover wet-season ranges measuring hundreds of square kilometres. The magnificent black sable bulls are territorial and defend their territories against intruding males. In order to mate they wait for female herds to pass through. Unlike female zebras in harems, sable females are independent and pass through the territories of many bulls in their seasonal wanderings. Young males leave the female herds and form bachelor groups, waiting to establish their own territories when they are large enough to challenge a resident male. Only the fittest males obtain a territory and have the chance to breed.

By June or July, in the middle of the cold dry season, the mopane woodlands have changed dramatically, resembling autumnal beech woods in Europe. The leaves have dried to gold and russet colours which match the papery kidney-shaped seed pods that cover the trees. Wind scatters the dying leaves and dry seed pods. In the sandveldt the pans have long since dried, the grasses are gone and the shrubs and most trees have lost their leaves.

Ecologically, mopane woodlands are at their most important at this time. Mopanes are among the last trees to drop their leaves, which are rich in protein and phosphorus and more palatable in this condition than when green, thus a source of winter food. Elephants relish them and reach high to break off branches, bringing leaves within the reach of smaller animals. Buffaloes, kudus, impalas and sables all feed on the drying leaves. Giraffes sometimes abandon arid acacia grasslands and move to mopane woodlands to feed on the late crop of leaves, their patterned coats a perfect foil against the gold and grey of the mopane trees.

On its 80-kilometre journey through the Panhandle, the Okavango River meanders through papyrus swamps contained between two parallel faults.

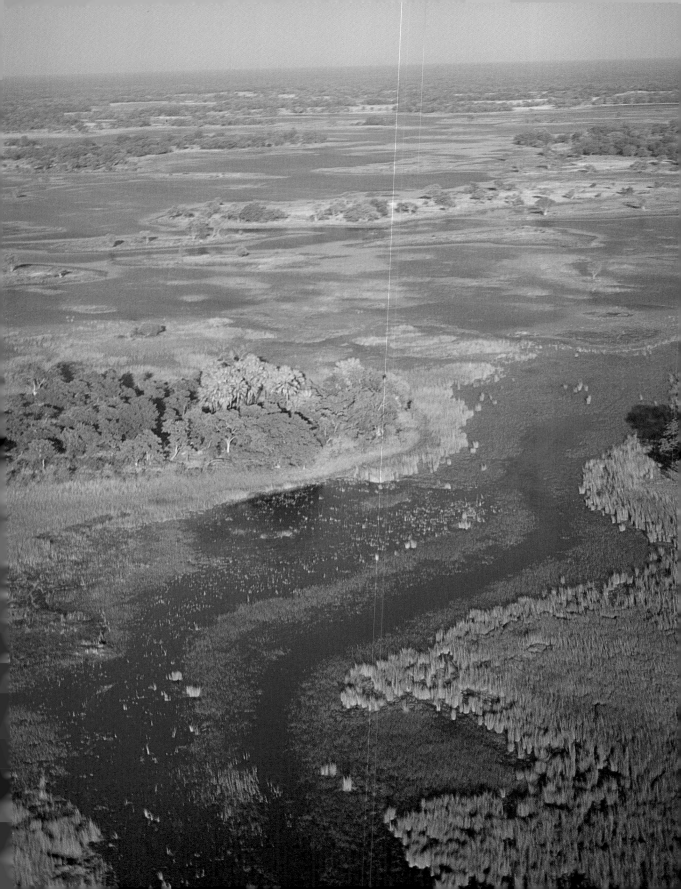

On leaving the Panhandle, the Okavango's waters spread out over the Kalahari sands (opposite), transforming the 'desert'. In spite of its luxuriant growth, papyrus (this page, top), is inhabited by relatively few creatures. A freshwater shrimp (bottom) survives in the peaty water by feeding on detritus trapped by papyrus roots.

Hippopotamuses (this page, top) and crocodiles (bottom) are the largest animals occurring in the Panhandle. African skimmers nest on sandbanks in the Okavango River (opposite), exposed during periods of low water.
OVERLEAF: *At dusk, skimmers cut a path through the water as they fish, lower beak snapping shut on contact with a fish.*

The sitatunga (below) is the only large mammal to inhabit the papyrus swamp. Its long hooves, which splay out as it walks, allow it to travel through the swamps with ease. Although the majestic fish eagle (opposite top and bottom), common throughout the Okavango Delta, is an adept fishing bird, it also scavenges on the catch of other creatures.

A Pel's fishing owl chick (top) sits beside its nest, the hollow fork of a large mokutshumo tree filled with bark chippings. A magnificent adult Pel's owl (bottom) drops from an overhanging branch into the water to catch a fish.

On leaving the restraining faults of the Panhandle the Okavango's waters spill and spread over the Kalahari sands, forming a vast delta of lagoons, channels and reedbeds.

Life abounds in the shallow, reedy backwater lagoons (opposite). Here carnivorous sundews (this page, top left) catch insects such as dragonflies (top right). The bell-like calls of the painted reed frog (bottom left) and the sonorous croak of the beautifully camouflaged back-striped Rana *frog (bottom right) dominate the night.*

In tranquil lagoons, water lilies (opposite top) support an intricate web of life. Pygmy geese (opposite bottom, left and right) feed on the seeds of lily bulbs. Midges lay eggs in a day lily flower (this page, top) while a carpenter bee collects pollen from a water lily (bottom right) and takes it to its nest in a hollow phragmites stem (bottom left).

The stamens of the day lily provide a meal for blister beetles (top). The yellow night lily (bottom left), like some other flowers, 'changes' sex to ensure cross-pollination; a visiting insect, carrying pollen from a male flower, falls into the stigmatic fluid of the female night lily (bottom right) and drowns.

Elephants dig holes in the clay mud to reach the moisture beneath, which collects to provide drinking water for other animals. Perhaps it is the drying pools that signal the passing of another season, but somehow the nomadic animals know that they must return to the rivers and swamps before the last waters evaporate. Gradually they set off, moving from pan to pan where there are hopefully a few patches of water to sustain them on their long journey. They carry with them mopane seeds, stuck to their hooves by clay mud and the sticky gum-glands of the pods themselves, thereby extending the range of this vital habitat. Mopane seeds germinate above ground, hence the meaning of their scientific name – 'seed of light'.

The exact destination of the different herds is still not known. Some return to the same dry-season refuge year after year; buffaloes, elephants and others wander more widely. Small scattered groups join as they journey. Thousands of animals travel to the fringes of the Delta, in anticipation of the annual floods. Many journey northwards to the waters of the Linyanti swamps and the Chobe River, which in prehistoric times joined the Okavango and Zambezi rivers to flow southwards into the Makgadikgadi pans.

By the end of the dry season there is an incredible diversity and abundance of life in the riverine forests that extend along the banks of all the major rivers – the Zambezi, Chobe, Linyanti and Okavango. Running parallel to the Chobe is a broad belt of *Brachystegia* woodlands. The animals must pass through these silent woods before reaching the blue waters of the river. Yellow and gold leaves fall in the cold wind and, except for the pistol-cracking of dry pods, the woods are silent. Sable and roan antelopes, zebras and wildebeests return to the river flood-plains, resting during the day in the fringe of shady forests. Buffaloes crowd on the flood-plains to quench their thirst and lay the dust of their long journey in the swiftly flowing waters. Hundreds of elephants wade into the water, their calves playing in their new-found luxury.

They join the river's permanent residents – hippos, crocodiles, Chobe bushbucks and birds, snakes and fishes. Lechwe, puku and waterbuck, three closely-related antelopes, co-exist on the floodplains, avoiding competition by their different choice of food. The shimmering blue waters contrast vividly with the grey land, the winter-flowering jessie bush a welcome splash of colour.

The dry season concentration of elephants along the Chobe River is an extraordinary sight, the highest density of elephants in the world. This results in heavy feeding pressure in the riverine forests, particularly on knobthorn acacia. As long as elephants have freedom of movement, however, they will head into the interior when thunder first signals rain, giving the forests respite. Elephants are an integral part of the ecological system, making food and water available to other animals. With a population of over 100 000 elephants in Botswana, it is vital that they be allowed to go their way unhindered.

CHAPTER FIVE

The Jewel

the Okavango Delta in Botswana is Africa's largest and most beautiful oasis. The Okavango River, which rises in the highlands of southern Angola, never reaches the sea; instead its waters empty over the sands of the Kalahari. Here the thirstland meets a blue-green wilderness of fresh water, emerald reedbeds and towering trees. It is a natural refuge and giant water-hole for the larger animals of the Kalahari. The water gives rise to many forms of life unexpected in a 'desert' such as this – fish of all sizes, crocodiles basking on the sands, wallowing hippopotamuses, and secretive swamp antelopes. One can only wonder at how the Okavango Delta came to be here, in some amazing accident of nature.

The Delta, really an alluvial fan, is the last surviving remnant of the great Lake Makgadikgadi. It is also closely associated with the Kwando-Linyanti-Chobe swamps and river systems to the north-east. Long ago the Okavango, Chobe, Kwando and Upper Zambezi waterways flowed as one massive river across the central Kalahari, to join the Limpopo River and flow onwards to the Indian Ocean. Earth movements that created

the rift of the Kalahari-Zimbabwe Axis impeded this flow, causing a damming back of the giant river and, as a result, the formation of a series of huge and complex swamps.

As the Okavango River left the Angolan highlands and entered the flatness of the Kalahari, it slowed and dropped its sediment load. Channels became blocked and the water sought other courses, continuing to deposit its sediments wherever it travelled. Over time, some two million tonnes of sand and debris were deposited, creating the Delta's characteristic fan shape.

The waters of the Okavango still cut paths through this built-up cone and deposit their sand load, causing channels to change continually. Superimposed on these changes were the climatic fluctuations of the last million years. In arid periods the complex swamps and waterways would recede; in wetter times myriad channels and waterways combined to form a vast river flowing into the former Lake Makgadikgadi.

Two parallel faults now control the direction in which the Okavango River enters the Delta, in an area called the Panhandle. Other faults, a continuation of the Great Rift Valley of East Africa, which runs south-west to north-east, also direct its exit southwards. As the Okavango flows over the Gomare Fault the slope of the land breaks it up into smaller channels that fan outwards. These are blocked by two southern faults, the Kunyere and the Thamalakane, which redirect the Delta's myriad channels. The Thamalakane Fault acts as a 200-kilometre-long natural dam; here the Boro River abruptly changes direction and forms the Boteti River, which flows eastwards through a break in the fault towards the Makgadikgadi pans. In the west, the Nghabe River goes south towards Lake Ngami, the river's flow now intermittent.

The formation of rifts caused the ponding back of the Okavango's waters. This earth movement occurred in the last million years along with more arid climatic phases. It accelerated the building of the cone-shaped Delta through further deposition. The same movement caused a ponding back of the Kwando river system, its waters escaping north-eastwards to join the Zambezi system via the Victoria Falls.

The present-day Okavango is still connected to the Chobe-Zambezi system via the Selinda Spillway but these water courses now seldom join. The geology of the Okavango is inherently unstable as faults continue to move and earth tremors occur, muffled by the deep sand. Channels come and go, filling with sediments while plugs of papyrus interrupt their flow. The pattern of drainage in the Delta continually changes, new swamps forming while others dry.

A freshwater delta

Rivers that do not reach the sea typically occur in arid areas where water evaporates to leave a saline pan, as in Makgadikgadi. The Okavango River is unique in that it is a freshwater drainage system. The Delta's rivers are born and die remarkably quickly, creating a mosaic of different stages of water distribution and ensuring the system remains dynamic. Changing channels help keep the waters fresh in spite of massive evaporation which deposits earth salts onto land. Dissolved salts can accumulate to toxic levels on sands islands, but rain washes them away after a channel dries, keeping the ground and water sweet.

There are two main outlets: west to Lake Ngami and south and east to the Makgadikgadi pans via the Boteti River. The flatness of the Delta gives rise to a very unstable drainage pattern, where any small change in the lie of the land causes a shift in water flow. For example, until the 1880s the Thaoge River to the west carried the bulk of the Okavango's flow as far as Lake Ngami. The strength of flow has now shifted, probably from a tilting of the earth's crust. The eastern rivers, the Moanatshira and Mborogha, carry far more water today than they did a hundred years ago. Little changed, the Boro River runs south-east through the heart of the Delta, skirting the western edge of a massive sand island called Chief's Island.

Two plants dominate the Delta's permanent swamps: papyrus, a giant sedge that grows naturally only in Africa, and the willowy *Phoenix* date palm. They provide a record of changes in the limits of the perennial waters. Papyrus, a herbaceous species, responds more quickly to changes in water level than the *Phoenix* palm.

The full extent of the Thaoge River, before it began to dry up, can be seen by the distribution of *Phoenix*, which extends much farther south than papyrus. Conversely, papyrus extends much farther east along the Moanatshira system, marking the expansion of perennial swamps in the last century. Papyrus and *Phoenix* occur in the same places on the Boro River, an indication that the river has been relatively stable in recent times.

The Panhandle

The Okavango River originates in the highlands of Angola as two tributaries, the Cubango and the Cuito. After several hundred kilometres, the Okavango is guided into the Delta's Panhandle between two northern faults about 15 kilometres apart. Here sand deposits have built up the river bed, causing water to spill and flood the land between the two faults as the river meanders widely between them. On a map the Panhandle looks like the northern 'wrist' of the many-fingered Delta 'hand'. This perennially flooded area is covered by dense reedbeds dominated by papyrus. Here the contrast between emerald-green plant life and the dry brown thornveldt of the Kalahari is dramatic.

Although the drainage pattern in the Delta is complex, there is an underlying simplicity in the slow and regular pulse of water that flows down each year from the Angolan highlands. South of the Panhandle the Delta fans out over at least 16 000 square kilometres. In wetter years, with a heavy annual flood, the Okavango's waters can spread over 20 000 square kilometres of the Kalahari's sands. Deep water occurs in a few channels while vast reedbeds are covered by only a few centimetres of water.

The 80-kilometre journey of the Okavango through the Panhandle is its last as a single river. Here it flows fast and wide, the rush and eddy of its strong current the only accompaniment to the twittering of birds. Between uncolonised areas of open water and the advancing papyrus there is a silent but continual battle. In the Panhandle the river's flow is strong enough to hold back the jungle growth and papyrus bends submissively over its banks, feathery heads dragged with the current.

Sometimes the river swings past a mainland spit, its edges lined by dense forests of fig, ebony and giant acacia. These are the daytime perches of fish eagles and the night roosts of fishing owls; genets and civets may also prowl here. The Panhandle is the domain of swamp specialists. Hippos, crocodiles and predatory fish live in the main channels while papyrus swamps have their own specialised animal life. Only the main Delta, with its larger islands and flooded grasslands, supports Africa's plains animals.

The luxuriant growth of papyrus is surprising, occurring as it does on impoverished Kalahari sands in waters that contain equally few nutrients. One of the fastest-growing plants on earth, it is able to absorb nutrients even when they occur in very low concentrations. Nitrogen comes from microscopic bacteria and algae found between the scale-leaves of papyrus, which take nitrogen from the air and make it available to the plant. The flood regime of the Delta, which allows for a period of dryness, is of great importance to the nutrient system of the swamps. Papyrus uses the specialised 'Carbon-4' pathway of photosynthesis, capturing the sun's light energy more effectively than most plants.

At the start of summer the spiky flower heads of papyrus, called 'umbels', produce thousands of seeds which fall into the river as they ripen and are swept downstream. Some become embedded in mud and germinate, but the plant generally grows and reproduces from its matted root and rhizome system which sends up new shoots at regular intervals. Shoots have an astonishingly short lifecycle, growing, maturing and dying within 90 days. As they die, the plant withdraws their nutrients and uses them for other shoots. This economy of nutrient cycling is a key to the rapacious growth of papyrus.

More and less at home in papyrus

Insects capitalise on the continuous dying and re-growth of papyrus shoots. Sap-sucking bugs such as aphids colonise them when they are young and green. As the papyrus matures its multiple spikes make homes for predatory insects like beetles and praying mantises, which feed on the aphids. When the umbels reach old age spiders spin webs in the spikes to trap mayflies and midges that have hatched from the water. There are thousands of other shoots to continuously replace those that die.

Papyrus is a difficult habitat for larger creatures. The dense stems tower overhead and are as tightly packed as an impenetrable jungle. The stems are fibrous and difficult to digest. The roots and rhizomes form floating mats that are so loose and spongy that any creature larger than a rat sinks through. In the water below, conditions are just as difficult for aquatic life. Little light penetrates through the jungle of stems and roots, and the continual dying of vegetation creates a build-up of acidic waters low in oxygen.

Several rodent species live in the reedbeds although none stays permanently in the soggy floating papyrus mats. Their burrows tend to be in the drier mats of aquatic grasses that are rooted on the banks of channels. Rodents feed on the shoots of young papyrus and reeds. The largest is the greater cane rat, which is surpassed in size only by the dry-land porcupine.

Cane rats live in family groups. When alarmed, the male warns his family by whistling loudly and thumping his back feet. They can swim but usually forage on land, forming tunnels, or 'runs', through fallen reeds and grasses, which hides them and make travelling through reedbeds much easier. Smaller aquatic rodents – the large vlei rat and shaggy swamp rat – share their runs.

The creatures most at home in papyrus are birds, which are able to fly over its vast swamps. They use the reeds to hide and build nests in and, occasionally, as food. Weavers and red bishops tear the rays off umbels to weave their domed nests. The plucked papyrus heads make good vantage points from which to display to females. Each red bishop male mates with up to seven females, calling and displaying in his brilliant red breeding after he has built the main structures of several nests. The females line the nests with soft grass flowers. They incubate the eggs and feed the young while the male defends the territory.

Some birds use papyrus reeds simply as a handy perch or resting place while on a journey. On occasion the coppery-tailed coucal can be seen sunning itself on the top of a mass of papyrus umbels. A secretive bird, its deep bubbling call, like water pouring from a jug, is an evocative early-morning sound in the Delta.

Nesting in papyrus obviously protects against larger predators, but snakes such as the boomslang move easily through reeds to rob nests of chicks and eggs. The coucal is also a notorious killer of nestlings it finds during skulking trips. Swamp birds like the little bittern are superbly camouflaged as they stand frozen, beaks reaching skywards, the stripes on their necks like the fluted stems of reeds. Pied and malachite kingfishers and goliath, squacco, green-backed and other herons are among the many birds that frequent the edges of papyrus, fishing in the main channel.

The dark, peaty root mats of papyrus beds demand unusual adaptations. The water bug compensates for low oxygen by pushing its small breathing tube above the water and sucking up air which it traps beneath its wing covers for use when hunting dragonfly larvae underwater. The larvae of lake flies live in the muddy bottom of inner swamps during the daytime, migrating to the surface at night to feed on plankton. Insect larvae are food for fish, which follow them to the surface at night or take the pupae when they are about to hatch.

Papyrus root mats are safe places for smaller fish to hide from predators: tiger fish, voracious sharp-toothed catfish and crocodiles. The spiny eel, named for the tiny row of spines along the back, lives among the fine root hairs of papyrus rhizomes where the water is better oxygenated, feeding on small freshwater shrimps which are abundant in papyrus roots.

Smaller species of fish, such as the thin-faced bream, and juveniles of larger species hide in papyrus edging the main channels. A strange-looking mormyrid known as the bulldog fish takes refuge in the roots by day, coming out only at night to feed in open backwaters. Bulldog fish communicate by weak electrical signals, feeling for prey in the mud with their strange, fleshy, bulbous lower jaw.

The high-acidity and low-oxygen levels of the papyrus swamps are intolerable to the Delta's largest predatory fish, the tiger fish. The swiftly-flowing main channels and large lagoons in the

Upper Delta are the domain of this relative of the piranha. As the floods subside and smaller fish and juveniles of larger species leave the floodplains and reedbeds to return to the main system, they are heavily preyed on by tiger fish.

The shy and elusive sitatunga

A swamp antelope, the sitatunga, is the only large mammal able to inhabit papyrus reedbeds and feed in them. The sitatunga occurs in swampy habitats in central and eastern Africa, the Okavango Delta marking its most southerly distribution. It occurs widely in the perennial Delta swamps but probably reaches its highest concentration in the abundant swamp habitat of the Panhandle and Jao flats.

Related to bushbuck and kudu, the male sitatunga has the impressive curved horns that characterise the Tragelaphine family of antelopes. A large species, males weighing over a hundred kilograms, the sitatunga can traverse matted reedbeds and soft marshy ground with ease because of its elongated hooves (nearly twice the usual length of antelope hooves) that splay out as it walks. Like other antelopes living in thick cover, sitatungas have raised hindquarters, which gives them a slow, loping gait and allows them to force their way carefully through dense reeds with the minimum of noise.

The shy nature of sitatungas is, perhaps, a reflection of the habitat they live in. Essentially solitary, they occasionally form temporary feeding groups of six or more individuals. The strongest social tie is between the female and her young, who will remain together until the calf is three-quarters grown. Sitatunga calves are born on a platform of flattened reeds deep in papyrus beds and remain hidden in this refuge for many weeks, the female visiting twice a day to suckle her calf. The young have a 'hiding' instinct and remain motionless if a predator comes close.

Sitatungas feed mainly in the early morning and evening, following well-worn and inter-connected pathways through papyrus to their feeding areas. They avoid hippo channels, which are used by large crocodiles, and are attracted to burnt areas where the new reed shoots are more palatable and nutritious. Their diet and movements are dictated by the fluctuating water level of the flood regime.

During periods of high water sitatungas move nearer dry land, where a wider variety of foods is available. When the water level is low, they move deep into the central swamps, existing mainly on young shoots of papyrus and their feathery tops. This antelope will reach up and hook a tall stem beneath its outstretched chin and bite halfway through the stem to bend it and bring the umbels within reach, making a loud popping sound.

In the day sitatungas lie on a platform of papyrus stems flattened by trampling or on a grass island in the cool shallow waters of a quiet lagoon, often moving their resting places so that predators cannot discover them. When alarmed the male slinks through the reedbeds with chin held high and horns resting along his back to prevent the horns becoming entangled in the dense vegetation. If threatened, sitatungas sink low into the floating papyrus mats and freeze, remarkably well camouflaged by their shaggy brown coats. When in danger in open water, they sometimes sink under with only their nostrils above the surface of the water. Although young sitatungas are taken by pythons, and adults are sometimes preyed on by lions on the islands, their main predators are crocodiles.

Baskers and skimmers

Crocodiles in the Panhandle reach an enormous size, some as much as five metres long and of considerable strength. Still and prehistoric, they bask on the sandbanks of the wide Okavango River as it meanders south to an uncertain destination.

Female crocodiles lay their eggs in sand when water levels drop and the sandbanks are exposed, secluded from the main river by papyrus and reeds. The eggs hatch in January before the water rises with the floods. The incubation period is 90 days, the female remaining nearby to protect the eggs from nest-robbers such as the Nile monitor.

As the eggs hatch she uncovers them and gently takes the young in her mouth, carrying them to water. The rise in water level ensures that new small pools are available to them, away from the dangerous main channel. Such maternal care seems surprising in such an ancient creature, which has remained almost unchanged for 200 million years. Young crocodiles feed mainly on

insects, in particular dragonflies, which they snap neatly from reeds and sedges, and on giant water bugs and freshwater crabs. Few survive their numerous predators, including vultures, monitor lizards, the sharp-toothed catfish and man. As they increase in size the young begin to hunt catfish and bream and other fish. Although often killed by the lethal barbs of catfish 'squeakers', they most often take these fish.

When over two metres in length, crocodiles begin to hunt mammals, in particular antelopes, goats and cattle. In the Panhandle many cattle graze along the exposed floodplains during low water, a rich food source that accounts for the extraordinary size and girth of some crocodiles! As sandbanks do not occur in the Delta proper, the Panhandle is the Okavango's crocodile population's major breeding ground, from where they migrate to new feeding areas in the Delta. Research indicates that human disturbance of their breeding grounds is threatening the species.

Exposed sandbanks are also important to migratory African skimmers, which fly south to the Panhandle to breed during the period of low water. After an elaborate courtship display, the pair mates. Their eggs are laid in a shallow depression in the sand, male and female taking turns to incubate them in the blazing sun, cooling them with breast feathers immersed in the river. Skimmers are a lovely sight as they fly gracefully over the wide river. Their long wing-span holds them aloft as they skim a few centimetres above water, the lower beak cutting a trail through the surface.

The 'Catfish Run'

Every year, just before the floods, thousands of catfish migrate up the main channels of the Okavango towards the Panhandle. The 'Catfish Run' is a unique phenomenon which has probably evolved in response to the annual floods. It is an intensive feeding period for catfish during low water, just before they move out onto the floodplains to spawn during the floods in January. As many as four distinct catfish runs a day may take place simultaneously in different areas during the peak of the run in October.

The travelling catfish hunt along banks of papyrus, where they thrash their bodies against the plants and frighten hiding fish out into the main river. Even from afar, the water seems to boil with the frenzied activity. The fish cover two to four kilometres per day, gradually moving upstream. The main species is the sharp-toothed catfish, a fierce predator over a metre in length, which congregates in big shoals at this time of year. It is joined by the blunt-toothed catfish, which moves into the Delta's main channels from the drying floodplains as the Lower Delta's waters recede, changing its diet from shellfish to fish.

The Catfish Run attracts huge flocks of fish-eating birds such as fish eagles, cormorants, darters, herons, kingfishers and egrets that follow the hunting shoals. The run also attracts crocodiles and snakes, while tiger fish at the periphery snap up fish as they are flushed from their papyrus refuge, locating bulldog fish by electrical signals the bulldogs discharge in fright.

Night life

During the day the swamps are quiet apart from the calls of birds such as coot-like gallinules or pied kingfishers. As dusk falls the cricket chorus begins, punctuated by the chimes of reed frogs and the croaking of toads. African skimmers cut a path with their beak through the mercury-smooth waters of the Okavango. The strange popping sound of papyrus stems breaking under the teeth of sitatungas is sometimes heard deep in the swamps.

After a full moon, the surface of the river and the warm swamp air are alive with millions of swarming lunar mayflies. Whiskered terns swoop over the water to feed on the winged adult flies that live for a few hours, mating before they die.

The magnificent rufous-coloured Pel's fishing owl roosts in the tall mokutshumo (African ebony) and fig trees on the banks. As darkness falls it leaves its roosts to perch on the branch of a large tree a metre or two above the water. On sighting a passing fish the bird swoops or, more literally, drops into the water, feet-first, with eyes shut at the moment of impact. The long curved claws and tiny spines on the undersides of the feet grasp the slippery fish and, with a massive beating of its wings, it lifts itself and the fish out of the water. The nocturnal habits of the owl and the diurnal habits of the formidable fish eagle enable both to live here in relative harmony.

The Pel's fishing owl is a secretive bird. Its booming call in the night in the hours before dawn is part of the magic of the Okavango.

6

CHAPTER SIX

Place of Reeds

dawn arrives quietly in the reed-lined channels. Towering walls of papyrus block out the sun's early morning rays. The river, still in shadow, glistens like oil as it slides and eddies along its relentless course, the mists of early morning rising from its surface. The only evidence of the channel's strong flow is the curve and rustle of floating hippo grass as the water sweeps by. The land is so flat that the first rays of sunshine fall first on palms, standing tall above the reeds on the occasional termite mound, dark fronds etched against a cobalt sky like frozen fountains. By seven o'clock the sun has climbed high enough to reach the western banks of the channels, filling the reedbeds with filtered light. Suddenly the place is alive with the songs of birds.

The moment the Okavango River leaves the restraining arms of the Panhandle it spills and spreads over the Kalahari sands in a fan-shaped delta, dominated by swampland in its upper reaches. A few main channels carry the bulk of the Okavango's water through the Delta like great aqueducts. Some travel south, others flow east until a fault line in the landscape re-directs

them southwards again. The occasional lagoon reaches a depth of several metres, but only the main channels bear a resemblance to the former Okavango River. Some 20 to 30 metres wide and up to 5 metres deep, the channel beds are sandy and, owing to the swiftness of the current, are largely devoid of vegetation. These channels pump the Okavango's waters through the Delta before they are lost to the sun.

The northern Delta is covered by shallow water, flooded grasslands, backwater swamps, oxbow lakes and hidden lagoons inter-connected by narrow waterways. The region is a complex of perennial and seasonal swamps and floodplain grasslands. The seasonal swamps are flooded after the annual floods when the rivers spill their banks and inundate vast tracts of land – just where depends on rainfall and the direction and intensity of the river's flow that year. Change is of the essence in the Okavango waterways.

Papyrus is ousted by phragmites reeds and sedges as the swamps become less permanent. Miscanthus grass occurs in shallow flooded sites and occupies vast areas called flats in the middle of the Delta, growing in thick tussocks, some three or four metres high. It is virtually impenetrable. Miscanthus is one of the first plants to colonise deposits of sediment or peat accumulation and as such plays a major role in the gradual change from swamp to floodplain. However only a few creatures, such as nesting birds, can make use of its long, spiky leaves.

Tall reeds and carpenter bees

Bullrushes are the least abundant of the tall reeds, but grow in patches in shallow lagoons and backwater swamps. Tall strap-like leaves provide a more open habitat, permitting the delicate *Nymphoides* snow-lily to spread over the water's surface and grow in their dappled light. Phragmites dominate the sluggish waters of medium depth, where they fringe river channels away from papyrus areas. They are the tallest of the swamp plants, towering five metres above the water. Elephants can eat only their fibrous root system; the tall bamboo-like stems are inedible even to those giants.

The dry hollow stems provide the perfect home, however, for the industrious carpenter bee. The female bores a hole in the stem and polishes and smooths the inside to make a nest. The shavings provide a 'plug' with which she partitions off each egg as it is laid along the stem. In each cell she leaves a ball of pollen and nectar, food for the developing larva. Water lilies are the bees' most abundant food source, but when the flowers die in winter the bees travel to islands to visit sausage trees and other winter flowerers.

There are many predators of the carpenter bee. Against the yellow bee-pirate wasp it has little defence. The wasp waits, often well camouflaged in a yellow night lily (*Nymphaea lotus*), ready to pounce on a visiting bee and sting it to death. In true pirate spirit the wasp squeezes the dead bee to extract every drop of fluid and nectar before flying off with the carcass, in which it will lay its eggs. The bee's home is generally safe from other attacks, but a fallen reed may form a 'bridge' along which the tiny but voracious brown ant can invade. However, the bee inside the reed can block the circular entrance with its abdomen, which seems tailor-made for the purpose.

Negotiating the maze

Apart from the main channels, the water appears almost directionless as it spreads over the flat Kalahari sands. Some channels lead to hidden lagoons, others are lost in a maze of thick towering reeds, all the waters in truth connected as they pass through reedbeds on their southward journey.

Humans still travel these channels best in the traditional wooden dug-out canoe, the 'mokoro', brought here by the BaYei people of the Zambezi when they discovered the Delta several hundred years ago. Even with a mokoro, however, progress is stopped suddenly by a thick plug of vegetation. A pair of pygmy geese, meanwhile, may fly overhead with frustrating ease, landing on a lily-covered lagoon only metres beyond the impenetrable wall.

Airborne creatures are the true masters of the Okavango. They fly over the banks of reeds, use the fibrous stems and unpalatable leaves for nests and homes, and travel effortlessly from lagoon to backwater to island in search of food. They are by far the most abundant and diverse creatures in the Okavango: birds, dragonflies, mayflies, midges and bees fill the air with their comings and goings and vibrant colours. The nocturnal dragonfly swoops low along the waterways at dusk; in the fading light its huge iridescent eyes spot the midges on which it feeds. At night small bats swoop along the narrow channels, scooping moths and insects from the water surface.

Leaving the Panhandle, the waters of the Okavango tend towards murkiness, coloured by peaty debris and carrying massive sand loads. The Delta's vast expanses of reedbeds act as a filter, slowing the water so that the sediments are deposited. In the lagoons the water, diverted from the swift main channel, forms tranquil lakes where the current is slow enough to allow the establishment of underwater plants. Some are ox-bow lakes – 'madiba' – cut off from the main channel by ever-changing patterns of reedbeds.

Fish specialists

The majority of the 90 fish species in the Delta are herbivorous. Most feed on small particles, detritus and algae. The red-breasted bream, which abounds in lagoons is a specialist of flowering water plants, new lily leaves being a partic-ularly favoured food. Predatory fish are less abundant although the tiger fish lives in lagoons – a powerful hunter with a vicious set of large conical teeth. Striped robber fish are among its prey, as are cichlid fish too large to escape to the safety of backwater swamps. Tiger fish take catfish and have been found with even poisonous snakes in their stomachs.

One of the few fish that is able to live alongside the tiger fish is the 'squeaker', a relatively small catfish whose name comes from the grating sound it makes when disturbed. Squeakers are well protected by sharply barbed spines on each of their dorsal and pectoral fins, which can be locked into a completely rigid position. Small crocodiles and tiger fish have been found dead with the three-pronged barbs of a squeaker locked firmly in their gullets.

The squeaker is nocturnal. It feeds upside down and uses its finely divided sensory barbels ('whiskers') to detect insect larvae and worms. By day it remains hidden beneath logs, where many squeakers will hide together. Being sluggish they are easy prey for the reed cormorant and form its major food source. The reed cormorant has a unique method of immobilising the squeaker. It dives underwater, searching beneath logs to locate the fish and bringing it up to the surface in its beak. Here it manipulates the squeaker until it can thrust its lower beak into the fish's head from behind, through the gills. This technique kills the squeaker before it is able to erect and lock its fatal barbs.

Lagoon life

The clear waters and open expanses of lagoons are the most beautiful and peaceful places in the Okavango – the realm of the fish eagle. These birds usually pair for life, each pair defending a territory that includes a sizeable stretch of water and suitable trees for nesting and perching. They attack trespassing eagles near the ground, although in the 'upper air' all individuals may soar and glide freely. Their haunting cries as they perch majestically on the branch of a favourite tree are one of the most evocative sounds of the Delta. Fish eagles hunt tiger fish, large bream and pike, but are not above scavenging the kills of other creatures when the opportunity arises.

The low-nutrient Okavango waters gives rise in abundance to a submerged plant, the bladder-wort. A 'very aberrant organism', it is rootless and shows little distinction between leaf and stem. Thousands of air-filled bladders that trap its food – mosquito larvae – are the secret of its success. The mouth of each bladder has several tiny bristles that cause it to expel water when touched by a passing animal, creating a suction effect which draws in tiny creatures. These are digested by microbes living in the bladder trap and enzymes the plant secretes. The plant's carnivorous habit gives it nutrients and reduces the number of mosquitoes that infest this swampy world.

Lagoons are fringed by water lilies and the white-flowering water chestnut. These aquatic plants thrive where the main stream slows to enter a lagoon and deposits its sediment load.

The water chestnut's rosette of heart-shaped surface leaves is held up by air bladders which act as flotation chambers. The most unusual feature of the plant is the seed pod armed with massive two-pronged barbs. These stick as an aid to dispersal of the edible seed within, their size indicating one dispersal agent in particular – the hippopotamus. Only the hide of the great 'water horse' would require a barb of this size to penetrate it!

Hippos are among Africa's most dangerous animals. They live in mixed herds, cooling off in water during the day and moving out to islands at night to graze. As they travel along well-worn paths, prominent trees are frequently dung-marked by the dominant male to proclaim his territory. The daily movement of hippos from lagoons through swampland to islands creates pathways through otherwise impenetrable reeds. These 'hippo paths' are used by many, including man, and help to make the swamps navigable.

Otters commonly occur in lagoons. There are two species in the Delta, the larger Cape claw-less otter and the spotted-necked otter. The enchanting spotted-necked otter is more common in remote lagoons where it spends most of the time in water, its streamlined and slender body design so adapted to water that it moves clumsily and slowly on land.

Family parties of otters are often seen porpoising through the water as they hunt for fish, frogs and crabs. A catch is usually consumed on the spot, prey clasped between forepaws as the otter floats on its back. An otter may suddenly disappear through a wall of papyrus. Behind this seemingly solid barrier lies an important part of the Delta – the shallow swamps that back open lagoons, constantly recharged with fresh clear water from the main system. Backwaters have small hummocks of land, forming islets where otters can secretly bask and play.

Backwater swamps

Densely covered by reeds, sedges and lilies, the backwaters contain a myriad small creatures. The competition between them is no less vibrant or dramatic than among the herds on the grasslands: the eternal struggle to eat and avoid being eaten while successfully breeding for the future.

In the summer months, from September to April, the backwater swamps are full of frogs, dragonflies, fish and insects. Mosquito larvae feed in the warm waters and, in turn, are food for an intricate web of carnivores. Dragonfly and damsel-fly larvae, restricted to life under water until their metamorphosis into adults, are voracious feeders. Reed frogs are abundant in the back-water swamps, and the long reed frog – a minuscule pale-green amphibian that perches on long reeds – feeds almost exclusively on mosquitoes.

Male reed frogs begin calling in the early warmth of spring. With the first rains the females appear, attracted by the vocal males. On summer nights, the bell-like calls of the painted reed frog and the high-pitched squeaky rasp of the long reed frog can reach a deafening crescendo as the males vie for the attention of females. Long reed frog males are particularly pugnacious and fight viciously to maintain a place on a slender reed, clasped with the suction pads on the feet. When other males attempt to clamber up the reed, the caller attacks with a series of karate kicks, kidney punches, left hooks and body squeezes – a ferocious battle for a creature less than two centimetres long. The kicking legs and flailing arms stretch to twice that length, however. The victorious male claims the top of the reed and, puffing out a translucent green throat, signals his dominance until the next frenzied skirmish.

By day reed frogs, especially pale green long reed frogs, can barely be seen as they cling to a swaying reed or the edges of a water lily pad. The skin of the painted reed frog, well named for its colourful varied pattern of brown, pink and white, is sensitive to light intensity. In the noon-day heat the frogs curl into a tight ball and their skin fades to white to reflect heat.

The backwater swamps are a safer habitat for small fish than open lagoons. Abundant food in summer promotes rapid growth, but fish must cope with the low oxygen levels of warm water. Top-minnows do this by living near the surface, where oxygen levels are highest. Small fish, with large iridescent blue eyes, they feed on small insects that fall into the water. This lifestyle so close to the surface makes them vulnerable to predators such as malachite kingfishers, which commonly dive for top-minnows. Their most unusual predator is the fishing spider, which has long slender legs well adapted to catching its prey. Its rear limbs have small hooks with which it anchors itself to a lily pad. Body and front legs then float motionless on water, ready to scoop up a passing top-minnow.

The fishing spider kills its prey immediately with a powerful poisonous bite that dissolves the fish's flesh, enabling the spider to suck in the juices. A spider can seize a fish up to twice its size and in the ensuing struggle may be carried underwater until the prey finally succumbs. Summer food brings the female into breeding condition. She does not mate every time, and can store sperm from one mating for months or even years. She carries the developing eggs on her back in a ball spun with silk, and during this time does not feed. When the eggs hatch she anchors the ball to a plant and spreads out the silk with her front feet, releasing hundreds of tiny spiders. The spiderlings are left to fend for themselves, though the ball acts as a web to trap tiny insects.

Backwater swamps are important nurseries for fish, while some species spend their entire lives there. The jewel cichlid, one of the most colourful fish in the Okavango, spawns on the stems of lilies and reeds, pairs defending their chosen site. For days after laying and fertilising their eggs, they fan water over them to increase the oxygen supply. When the eggs hatch the female moves the young to a clean depression in the sand, picking them up with her mouth and spitting them into the nest while the male stands guard. Threads on their heads attach the young to sand, and they circulate water by wriggling their tails. They become free-swimming as they grow, but remain with their parents for several weeks while searching for food in new areas.

The dwarf mouthbrooder is another cichlid distinguished by its breeding behaviour. Prior to breeding in summer the male becomes brightly coloured and, after establishing his territory on the swamp bottom, attracts a female by flashing and shimmering his colours. He fertilises the eggs as she lays them and then takes them into her mouth. The female bites near the male's anal fin to take sperm from his vent into her mouth and improve the chance of fertilisation. Keeping the eggs in her mouth, she churns them from time to time to keep them aerated. They hatch in five days, but the young remain in her mouth until they have absorbed their yolk sac.

During this time the female cannot feed. Her body becomes very thin and her distended mouth gives her a strange appearance. Once released the young forage around her and, although she routinely chases off other fish, she signals for them to return to the safety of her mouth when danger threatens. Mouthbrooding has its benefits in the shallow swamps where eggs are heavily preyed on, but this form of protection has its price. If the female is caught, so too is her entire family. One predator likely to take a cichlid family is the striped swamp snake. Truly aquatic, it ambushes prey under water by coiling itself around an underwater stem.

Night lilies and day lilies

Water lilies cover much of the Okavango's open water and when they flower in summer are a most languid sight. The symmetry of tall reeds balances the soft curves of lily leaves and the blue of the sky is reflected in the sparkling water with the bright blues, pale pinks and yellows of the flowers. In gusts of wind upturned leaves flash purple and green. Submerged lily stems can be seen clearly through the clear water, coiled like springs with small buds of unopened flowers at their tips ready to rise above the surface.

The base of a lily plant consists of a swollen rhizome, called 'tswee' – a delicacy for people living in the Delta. The long stalks of water lilies contain air canals that keep them afloat and help with the exchange of gases vital to the plant's respiration. The lily stem grows until the bud is above the surface, where it blossoms. After four to six days, the stalk of the lily retracts spirally pulling the flower back into the water where the fruit ripens and eventually disintegrates, releasing tiny red seeds.

There are two main species of water lily in the Okavango. The day-flowering *Nymphae caerulea* grows in shallow still waters throughout the Delta, its flowers appearing in a range of colours, from dark blue to pink and white. The yellow night lily *Nymphaea lotus* occurs in the deeper waters of channels and around the fringes of larger lagoons. Its lily pads have serrated edges and its flowers are less finely structured than those of the day lily.

Like many flowers water lilies have evolved a system to encourage cross-pollination. The male and female parts of the flower ripen at different times. When the flower first opens, the female ovules at the base are ripe but the male stamens do not yet bear pollen and visiting insects fertilise the flower with pollen from another plant. The night lily takes this one step further. It traps the visiting insect within its flower, using a device nothing short of murder.

During the 'female' stage the base of the night lily's flower contains a sticky fluid, above which the male stamens form a domed hood. An insect visiting the flower will fly into the hood, slide down the slippery sides of the stamens, and land in the fluid, unable to escape from the domed hood. The ensuing struggle ensures that any pollen on the insect falls into the fluid of the female bowl and so fertilises the flower. On subsequent days, when the flower is male and bears pollen, the hood of stamens is more open and the fluid dries up. Visiting insects can come and go freely, taking with them pollen to a receptive female flower elsewhere.

The night lily is a narcotic, its creamy yellow flower one of the most exotic blooms of the Delta. Its night blossoming suggests it has some mysterious mode of pollination – perhaps by dusk-flying midges attracted by the warmth and pungent fragrance. The opening times of night lily flowers are also unfathomed. When a flower first appears it opens at midnight and closes at around eight in the morning. On the second day

A female fishing spider (top) releases her young from their silk nest. The bladder-wort (bottom left), a carnivorous aquatic plant found in lagoons, traps mosquito larvae (bottom right) in thousands of tiny underwater air bladders.

The backwater swamps are important breeding areas for cichlid fish. Jewel cichlid pairs (top) share in raising their young. The male dwarf mouthbrooder (bottom) attracts a mate by 'shimmering'; after the female has taken the fertilised eggs in her mouth he plays no further reproductive role.

Reed cormorants (this page, top) hunt under submerged logs for catfish 'squeakers'. Even the voracious tiger fish (bottom) is in danger from the fin spines of squeakers, but cormorants are able to unlock the fish's spines before swallowing it. The striped swamp snake (opposite) coils around a reed to ambush its prey.

The foam nests of African pike (opposite top and bottom) hold their eggs above the murky waters. On hatching, the fry remain attached to the foam (this page, top), living off their yolk sac until large enough to swim freely and hunt small prey such as mosquito larvae (bottom). **OVERLEAF:** *Sunset over Xugana Lagoon.*

Fringing the Delta's numerous islands (opposite top) are thick groves of trees such as the strangler fig (opposite bottom) and the knobthorn acacia (this page, top). The well-camouflaged giant stick insect (this page, bottom) feeds on the new leaves and catkins of the knobthorn.

Island trees support an intricate web of life. Peters' epauletted fruit bats roost in a shady motsaudi tree (this page, top) and feed at night on ripe sycamore figs (opposite). The sweet fruits of the mokutshumo tree attract numerous birds including the green pigeon (this page, bottom).

A white-browed coucal (below) warms itself in morning sunshine. The flap-necked chameleon (opposite) is common on flowering motsaudi trees, where, moving gently like a fluttering leaf, it lies in wait for visiting insects which it catches with its long sticky tongue.

it opens earlier in the evening and remains open until seven the next morning. Subsequently it opens at about four in the afternoon and closes at midnight. If there is a reason for this strange pattern of opening and closing it is still a closely guarded secret.

Birds in lily-covered lagoons

Midge larvae laid in day lily flowers manufacture haemoglobin to increase their oxygen supply and become red. The red larvae, called 'bloodworms', are a favourite food of the lilytrotter, or African jacana, which steps lightly from pad to pad with its extremely long toes, foraging for insects. The jacana's breeding behaviour is unusual in that it is the male that raises the chicks. The female attracts her mate by starting a nest on a pad of floating vegetation. After mating and egg laying, it is the male who incubates the eggs and raises the chicks. The female leaves to look for another mate.

When the eggs hatch the male jacana hides the shells under lily pads so as not to attract predators. The precocious, gangling little chicks are able to leave the nest almost at once and feed on insects. Initially the male carries the chicks with him as he looks for food, putting them down from time to time. At the first hint of danger he crouches and calls the chicks to climb into his breast feathers. He makes a wonderful sight, stepping cautiously over lily pads with several pairs of stick-like legs protruding from his breast. If suddenly alarmed, the anxious father may accidentally drop the chicks into the water and the whole process has to be repeated.

The diminutive pygmy goose also graces the lily lagoons of the Okavango. The exquisite colouring and markings of the male – white, bottle-green and chestnut – are a perfect camouflage among the brilliant leaves and flowers of lilies. Pygmy geese live in pairs, flying fast and low over the water from lagoon to lagoon and resting on the surface as they converse in clear whistling calls. They feed almost exclusively on lily fruits. A goose will dive and peck the lily stem at a weak point just below the bulb to get a fruit. After several pecks the bulb breaks off the stem and the goose takes it to the surface, breaking it to get out the seeds. Before they are carried away by the current, spilled seeds are eaten by shoals of robber fish and bream.

Pygmy geese nest in the hollows of old trees or the abandoned nests of hamerkops. The female lays up to ten eggs in a down-filled hollow and the goslings leave their nest almost as soon as they hatch, fluttering down to the lily-covered waters of the lagoon from their nests in the trees.

7

CHAPTER SEVEN

Islands

Scattered throughout the Delta are millions of islands, dazzling in their numbers and variety. They rise just high enough above the surrounding reedbeds and floodplains to support the growth of trees. In the northern swamps islands are so small that there is room for only a single grove of the graceful *Phoenix* palm.

In the middle Delta islands become larger, narrowly edged with woodlands of lovely trees with lyrical Setswana names – mokutshumo, motsaodi, mokoba, motshaba. Each island is unique in the mix of trees it bears, with its own 'look' and atmosphere. Surrounded by water, the woodlands that fringe islands grow lofty and luxuriant with species like the sausage tree, fig tree, African ebony and the densely foliated African mangosteen (motsaodi) that could never otherwise survive on impoverished Kalahari sands.

Tall yellow-barked sycamore figs line the edges of islands, leaning over the waters of lagoons. Associated with the large figs that cluster on their trunks and branches is an intricate web of life. As with all figs, a tiny parasitic wasp is responsible for pollination, the minute female wasp laying her eggs inside the fruit through the narrow opening at the top and pollinating the flowers within. The larvae develop as the fruit ripens and emerge as adults from the enlarged opening, or ostiole, now open to fruit flies, weevils, beetles and other, non-pollinating, insects that lay their eggs in this nutrient-rich environment.

Ripe figs are eaten by green pigeons, black-collared barbets, bulbuls, tree rats, baboons and monkeys. Fallen fruit are taken in particular by the large purple-headed bream and red-breasted bream, which build their nests among the half-submerged roots of the fig tree. Smaller robber fish feed on fig pieces dropped by birds and fish.

Towards the lower end of the Delta are extensive islands of Kalahari sand, or sandveldt tongues, that penetrate deep into this oasis. Chief's Island, the largest, covers over 1 000 square kilometres and supports vegetation and animal life more typical of dry deciduous Kalahari woodlands. Salt pans are interspersed with mopane woodlands and acacia thornscrub in its arid interior, limiting the range of water-dependent animals. Larger islands are fringed by a wide margin of floodplain grassland, inundated each year by floods.

Termite islands

Most of the smaller islands owe their existence to those ancient and forever active architects and builders, termites. Their activity raises patches of land above the flatness of the land and their earth-moving endeavours enrich the soil, encouraging the growth of trees and providing a diversity of habitats. The shape of a termite mound depends on the termite species, the local climate and the nature of the soil. Of the 400 species in Africa, fungus termites are those responsible for building the castles that rise dramatically above islands in the Delta.

Termite islands play an important role in the pattern of water flow, particularly in seasonal swamps. Termitaria may be built in the narrow entrances to floodplains in the dry season. As they grow their bases join, the land surface thus rising and preventing the flow of water into the formerly flooded area. In time the dried floodplains, or 'madiba', are colonised by trees and the termites continue their work.

If several islands are close together, the joining of termitaria creates a larger island. In this way the lands of the Delta, as well as the waterways, are constantly changing. The island-building activities of termites are continuous. Mounds can be built in a very short time and a temporary flow of water away from an area can result in the appearance of a mound and the beginning of an island should the waters return.

Termites cement particles of sand using a mortar of fine clay and saliva as well as calate, a salt found on the edges of the sand islands. Mounds may be five metres high and shaped as cones, domes or irregular pinnacles. Far from being static, a healthy termite mound is continually enlarged and renewed. Networks of galleries, corridors and cavities within are homes for snakes such as the olive grass snake, rodents and lizards. One of the most unusual residents of termite mounds is the banded rubber frog, which can wriggle its way acrobatically through termitaria corridors with its sticky padded feet in search of prey. Mammals such as the warthog and spotted hyaena often use old and enlarged termitaria hollows as dens for their young.

Fungus termites are ghostly white in colour and cannot tolerate daylight. They forage only at night and build a complex network of mud-covered runways to places where they feed on dead wood and animal dung. The magnitude of the process is difficult to appreciate. An entire tree is occasionally covered in mud while it is slowly consumed by the termites inside. In this way termites remove vast quantities of old wood which is partially digested and used in the mound to build the combs on which their fungus gardens grow.

Fungi thrive on partially-digested remnants of wood, converting them into nutrients and vitamins – tasty mushrooms on which termites feed. The fungus beds are carefully tended to provide a constant supply of food for the colony. Termite workers also spread material from the fungus beds near the mound. It grows into delicious white mushrooms the size of a dinner plate. Termites themselves are at the base of a vast food chain. Lizards, insects and birds prey heavily on them and the list of mammals that take them is long: shrews, vervet monkeys, bush-babies, squirrels, side-striped jackals, genet cats, several species of mongoose and even humans, who throughout Africa relish termites. The pan-golin is one of the few termite specialists restricted to well-watered areas.

As the first rains soften the brick-hard mounds, winged termites, or alates, of both sexes leave the nest through passageways opened up by workers. They fly as far as they can in a nuptial flight before landing. On touch-down the female releases a pheromone from her waving abdomen. When a male approaches a female, the couple shed their wings and begin work on a new colony. Fungus termites fly at dusk, and as they emerge from the mound evening birds and bats swoop down to catch them.

Diminutive jewel-like malachite kingfishers, coloured in the greens and blues of the water-ways, commonly excavate their nests in the sides of termitaria. These tiny birds fly low over the water like missiles and have a wonderful 'punk' crest of feathers which they raise when alarmed or threatened. Since there are very few river banks in the Okavango Delta, termite mounds are important nesting sites for kingfishers.

As the warm weather approaches in September, malachites begin to breed. The male courts the female by feeding her delicate

morsels of fish. They then excavate their nest burrow together, the female laying a clutch of four to six small, white and perfectly round eggs. Both parents share in the incubation of the eggs and the feeding of the young. While one parent guards the nestlings, the other flies to a nearby backwater to catch top-minnows or reed frogs. On its return the male kingfisher perches near the burrow signalling its mate with a high-pitched call. Young kingfishers remain with one of the parents to learn to fish, perching on low reeds that stretch over the water.

There are over 500 species of birds in the Delta. Flying from island to island, birds have much greater ease of access than land-bound creatures, although elephants, buffaloes, spotted hyaenas and even lions may wade or swim between islands as they journey through the swamps.

Island trees

Island trees flower just before the rains. First is the knobthorn acacia, whose mass of small white blossoms is a lovely sight etched against the blue of the late winter sky. The fragrant flowers attract birds and insects such as the giant stick insect, over 20 centimetres long, which feeds on newly emerged catkins. Well-camouflaged, the spines on its body even mimic the thorns on the bark, from which the knobthorn gets its name.

Despite its spiny nature the knobthorn is relished by many species. Baboons and squirrels feed on the pods, while elephants enjoy the gum that exudes from fissures in the bark they strip off the tree. This damage makes trees susceptible to fire, but even when killed by fire they are useful nesting sites for woodpeckers and barbets. The scops owl is beautifully camouflaged against the trunk as it rests by day, motionless. Palatable grasses grow in the shade of knobthorn acacias, providing food for seed-eaters such as fire-finches.

The sausage tree flowers slightly later, its large burgundy flowers a foil to the new green leaves. Bumble bees and carpenter bees visit the goblet-shaped flowers, filled with nectar, and colourful sunbirds flash among them. The pungent smell of sausage tree flowers spreads through the warm night air, attracting nectar-feeding bats, thought to be among the tree's main pollinators. Flowers that are knocked to the ground collect the dew of dawn and creatures like vervet monkeys and tree squirrels can sip moisture from the fallen blossoms.

The sausage-shaped fruits, which give the tree its name, grow to a length at which only large creatures like elephants, giraffes and hippos can handle them. However, Meyer's parrots feed on seeds embedded deep within the fleshy fruits, patiently removing the pith – like taking the cob off the corn – before they can reach the seeds.

Of all the trees that fringe the edges of the Delta's islands, the motsaudi offers the deepest and coolest shade. Groves of motsaudi trees are famous as Livingstone's favourite camping places during his Okavango/Zambezi explorations,

hence their Latin name *Garcinia livingstonei*. The massed flowers, glistening with sticky nectar, are almost hidden in the dense foliage but their fragrance attracts insects. The round orange fruits of the motsaudi are deliciously bitter-sweet and are relished by many, including man. The flap-necked chameleon, easily camouflaged by taking on the shape and colour of a motsaudi leaf, feasts on the dragonflies that prey on clouds of midges during the tree's brief flowering period.

The mokutshumo, African ebony, is a giant of the island woodlands, growing to over 30 metres in height. The sturdy dark trunk typically forks into two main branches before spreading into a mass of lesser branches. In time the cleft between the main boughs becomes eroded, the resulting broad-based hollow often used by Pel's fishing owls to raise their chicks. The owls' nest is kept clean by the larvae of dermestes beetles, which consume insects attracted to the nest by fallen morsels of fish.

Date-flavoured, yellow mokutshumo fruits cover the tree after most other tree species have already fruited. Animals gather round the base of the tree to pick up fruits knocked down by elephants, baboons and fruit-eating birds such as green pigeons. Dung heaps of the African civet are liberally peppered with mokutshumo seeds, as is the dung of the side-striped jackal. The trees also provide humans with a valuable harvest – indigenous people collect its sweet fruits, which are dried like raisins and then stored.

The arrival of summer brings migratory lesser striped swallows to the Okavango, where their favourite nesting sites are the underside of stout tree branches. The swallow's bowl-shaped nest is made from moistened clay pellets, collected from the edges of termite mounds. Pairs work in the morning, one bird sitting in the half-finished nest while the other collects a beakful of building clay. At dusk large flocks of lesser striped swallows flit and glide over the lagoons as they hunt the evening swarms of midges.

At night the sycamore fig is again the site of activity. Fruit bats, of which there are many species in the Delta, leave their dark roosts in the canopies of motsaudi trees, detecting clusters of figs by sight and determining their ripeness by smell. Insect-eating bats locate their prey by using sound waves like radar, but fruit bats rely on their amazingly detailed binocular vision which can pick up separate images of an object and compare them to judge depth and distance.

The bats hover near fig clusters before selecting one on which to land. A single fruit bat can consume at least 20 large figs in a night. Hanging by its feet at its feeding roost, it slowly chews the fruit to extract the juices, spitting out the seeds. Female bats carry their young on feeding forays for the first few weeks, after which they leave them in the roost, returning at intervals for the infant to lick fruit juices from its mother's mouth.

Quite at home in the trees, the nocturnal rusty-spotted genet – a beautiful, small, cat-like carnivore – balances with the aid of its long striped tail. Although related to the mongoose, it is an agile climber with adaptations that are both feline and canine. It hunts a variety of creatures, but its most common prey are the tree rats that inhabit hollows of old fig and motsaudi trees.

On the ground and in the water

The shy, nocturnal African civet is closely related to the genets, although it looks quite different. It is twice the length of a genet and five times its weight. It is believed that the earliest prehistoric carnivores looked much like this heavy-set creature, neither cat nor dog. Predominantly black in colour, with blotches and bold white bars, it has long coarse fur and a ridge of hair that it can erect into a crest down its back. Like a dog, it has non-retractable claws and, as a result, is more or less confined to a life on the ground.

A more vocal predator on the Okavango's islands is the water mongoose which inhabits the fringes of swamps and the banks of streams and rivers and is generally solitary except when mating. Heavy-set, it has thick coarse fur that no doubt helps to keep it warm when swimming in the cold water. Crabs are its favourite food and it picks these crustaceans out of holes in the shallow banks of islands. Mating is accompanied by spine-chilling screeches and much spitting and growling, and the courting pair may meet several times in succession each night.

In the first light of dawn small animals travel along the moss-covered pathways that weave through matted grasses and sedges, following the water's edge. These are the foraging routes of the semi-aquatic swamp rat and insectivorous musk shrew. Musk shrews are primitive creatures resembling the first mammals on earth, some 200 million years ago. Tiny eyes and poor eyesight mean they must rely on a faceful of whiskers to detect vibrations of insect prey. Because of its large incisors the animal drinks by dipping its mouth in water and then raising its head and letting the liquid trickle down its throat.

The shrew has a very high metabolic rate and must feed frequently both day and night. The glands on the flanks of both sexes give musk shrews their name. Their heavy musk odour taints their flesh and they are seldom preyed on, except by owls. The so-called tiny musk shrew is probably the smallest mammal in the Okavango, weighing only six grams but needing nearly that weight of insects a day to keep it going.

Gomoti fig islands

The larger lagoons of the central delta, such as Gedikwe Lagoon, contain tree islands of the water fig, or gomoti fig, which grows in tangled thickets in shallow water. The tiny red berries, like other figs, are an important source of food, but more important is the role of the gomoti islands as breeding colonies for birds.

Yellow-billed and open-billed storks, several species of heron, marabou storks and ibises nest there, some 24 species having been recorded breeding on the islands in Gedikwe Lagoon. Birds congregate on the islands in spring and egg-laying

is completed before the rains. Species with longer incubation times, such as marabou storks and yellow-billed storks, are the first to breed. In a frenzy of activity the birds call, display, mate and build nests with grasses, leaves and twigs gathered from communal areas on nearby islands.

Marabou storks and yellow-billed storks construct nests on the canopy of the water fig, their body size making it easier perhaps to protect the chicks from raptors such as kites and tawny eagles. The densely tangled nature of water figs allows different birds to nest at different heights. Smaller and more vulnerable species such as purple herons and sacred ibises nest in the shade of lower regions. The heat is intense for birds nesting in the upper levels of the fig colony. They shade the eggs with outstretched wings, or cool them by regurgitating water or dragging wet weeds over them. An advantage of breeding on fig islands is that few land-base predators can invade the fig colony. Against the Nile monitor, however, there is little protection. It moves over and through tangled fig trees with the aid of strong sharp claws.

Open-billed storks follow areas of fire damage to find their favourite prey of mussels and snails, which inhabit submerged rhizomes of papyrus. Leaving the fig colony they circle above the islands to catch a thermal to carry them over the long distance to their feeding grounds. The Delta is truly the domain of creatures that can fly – over reedbeds, swamp lands and lagoons, from island to island.

CHAPTER EIGHT

Flooded Grasslands

reedbeds and islands give way to large tracts of grasslands interspersed with extensive tongues of sand as the Delta stretches and spreads through its lower reaches. Inundated seasonally by floods and rains, the grassed plains – called floodplains – get too wet to support woodlands and too dry for the lush growth of reedbeds. The grasslands are of great importance to the larger grazing mammals of northern Botswana. The diversity and abundance of wildlife is at its greatest here, where the Kalahari meets the Delta.

Antelopes of all kinds are the most numerous large mammals in the area. This is the southern-most distribution in Africa of the red lechwe, which occurs here in large numbers. Essentially a swamp antelope, though not quite as specialised as the sitatunga, red lechwes prefer the borders between water and grasslands, where they can graze on the young shoots of sedges and grasses growing in shallow waters. When alarmed they take readily to water, their powerful hindquarters giving them the edge over their main predators, lions, leopards, wild dogs – and humans. A group of red lechwes bounding through the shallow

waters of the floodplains, sending up sprays of water that sparkle in the sun, is the signature of the Okavango.

Lechwes are particularly vulnerable when the floodplains are dry, and so tend to move with the water. During high floods they move ahead of the waters, from the more permanent swamps onto the grasslands, and then retreat as the floods sub-side. The breeding season of the red lechwe coin-cides with the seasonal flooding pattern in the Delta from January to April (and the rains) so that the young are born just after the floods recede in September, leaving the floodplains green and lush. By day lechwes play and feed; at night they sleep away from the water's edge to avoid crocodiles.

Only adult male lechwes that hold territories can mate with females. Female herds are rela-tively independent and move from territory to territory as they choose, attracted by areas of better grazing. There is much competition, with fighting and displaying, to establish dominance. The strongest males hold the best territories, have the most access to females, and so pass on their genes in the classic style of natural selection. On the alert, a proud male lechwe surveys his territory from the elevation of a termite mound, his heavy chestnut coat a perfect foil to the tawny grass and silver-red miscanthus flowers.

Floodplain residents and migrants

The mosaic of floodplain vegetation depends on the pattern of flooding and on the occurrence of sand islands and termite mounds. Because of regular flooding, the dominant plants are water-tolerant grasses as well as sedges similar to papyrus in their coarseness and lack of nutrients and protein.

Reedbucks live in pairs in the thick vegetation, always near water. When a reedbuck sees a potential predator it will hide behind a clump of reeds, ducking its head low but with its hindquarters showing clearly. There can be few better examples of 'playing ostrich'! When conditions are at their driest other large herbivores such as buffaloes, zebras, wildebeests and impalas move in. They need to be closer to the ever-receding waters of the Delta as other grasslands become dry and overgrazed.

The grasslands on sandy soils are the last areas of the Delta to be flooded. These are typically backed by the woodlands of the northern Kalahari interior from where more and more grazing animals return to water as inland pans dry out. The arrival of the floods is important to dozens of large herbivore species – sable, kudu, wildebeest, tsessebe, giraffe, zebra, impala, buffalo and warthog. Adjacent to most islands, and often enclosed by riverine woodlands, are small patches of short sweet grasses on which hippos graze at night. Hippos are important agents of 'nutrient transfer' for they feed on land and defecate in water, where they cool off during the hot days. Territorial males frequently spray dung on their land-based territories.

Harvester termites collect and process sprays of hippo dung, which contain undigested fragments of their preferred grasses. There is a link between hippos, harvester termites and fungus termites, the erosion of whose mounds also contributes to the enrichment of floodplain soils.

Impalas and tsessebes inhabit the floodplains throughout the year, not following the floods like lechwes nor dispersing into the sand islands like buffaloes and zebras. Tsessebes, unlike their close relative the red hartebeest, are dependent on water and males live in permanent territories on the floodplains. Tsessebes look almost clown-like, with sloping hindquarters and the comical face of the hartebeest, but are remarkably fast and agile – the fastest of all antelopes. They are seldom killed by lions, although they fare less well against the efficient pack-hunting wild dog.

Impalas are common in the Delta and are frequently seen drifting into the dappled shade of mopane woodlands during the heat of day. Both grazers and browsers, their numbers are related to the amount of 'edge' area between open grasslands and wood and bushland. They are a gregarious species and their varied feeding habits enable them to occur in large numbers and high densities.

Vocal signals are important to impalas and there is much roaring amongst territorial males during the mating season in winter. They have scent glands on their foreheads, and the rubbing of bushes by males helps them to define their territories. Both sexes possess large scent glands on their heels. The scent is important in laying a trail that enables individuals to keep in contact in woodlands, where visibility is poor.

Impalas leaping spectacularly, bounding from side to side as they scatter through bushes when alarmed, are one of the thrilling sights of the Okavango. This characteristic jumping has a function beyond simply confusing pursuing predators. The momentum of the leaps establishes a general direction of flight for the herd. As the impalas leap they kick out their heels, causing the black-marked fetlock gland to expand and release a puff of scent into the air. This is easier for running animals to follow than a scent trail on the ground and helps the group to maintain contact. Despite this group cohesion, impalas are frequently taken by predators including lions, spotted hyaenas, leopards, cheetahs and wild dogs – they are truly the larder of Africa.

Large herds of Cape buffaloes wander the Delta throughout the year, their population – excluding dry-season migrants from the Chobe woodlands in the north – standing at about 20 000 animals. In the past decade, however, their numbers have declined dramatically. Buffaloes roam the interior of sand islands such as Chief's Island, where they obtain water from rain-filled pans. The abundance of water encourages fast growth of floodplain grasses, but these have less substance than the sweeter grasses of more arid sandy areas. The more dangerous buffaloes are lone males. Old bulls accidentally disturbed in the dense habitats they prefer are potentially lethal.

Buffaloes graze in sand islands and sandveldt tongues only during the rains. This seasonal availability of good grazing is responsible for their narrow birth 'peak' from January to March. Towards the end of the dry season they roam the mosaic of islands and floodplains in the seasonal swamps. The dry-season change to floodplain grasses and the large numbers of animals on relatively small areas cause them to rapidly lose condition.

Palms and sand islands

In the palm groves of sandy islands dry palm leaves rustle and scrape in the wind. A white-backed vulture circles overhead and lands on its eyrie in the tallest tree. *Hyphaene* palms tower overhead, their fan-shaped leaves etched against the blue sky, massive clusters of large shiny ginger-coloured fruits half hidden in the thick fronds. Filtered sunlight reflects on white sands sparsely covered by spiky grasses.

Palm groves here are like those in the famous Makgadikgadi palm belt deep in the Kalahari. There are many, scattered throughout the Delta on ridges of sand that rise above the transforming effects of water, retaining many of the characteristics of the arid Kalahari. There is one difference – an abundance of clear fresh water within easy walking distance.

The flooding regime affects only the fringes of the sand islands, some of which are several hundred square kilometres, leaving a narrow band of floodplain grasses along their edges. At this time the sandy edges of the narrow floodplains are covered with a soft white powder, like a snowfall. The powder is in fact a mass of salt crystals (sodium bicarbonate) that are earth salts brought to the surface and deposited as the water evaporates. Termites use calate, a by-product of this process, to build their mounds. The salts that accumulate from evaporation in this way are flushed away by the annual cycle of floods and rain. Couch grass, a remarkable African species, can tolerate the salinity of these areas. Few creatures make use of this saline habitat – one of them is the funnel-web spider which spins its web between salt-covered grass stems, waiting until a fly or midge falls into its camouflaged silk-lined tunnel.

A few metres inland the sands rise enough to avoid flooding and support woodlands of knobthorn and combretum trees. *Hyphaene* palm groves occur in areas where underground waters tend towards brackishness. Tracks in the loose sands tell of the creatures that move through the dryland woods and down to the water's edge to drink: the large round prints of elephants; prints of all sizes and shapes of cloven-hoofed animals such as giraffes, kudus,

impalas, buffaloes and warthogs; and pug marks that tell of the elusive presence of African carnivores – hyaenas, lions, leopards and small side-striped jackals.

Elephants love *Hyphaene* palm groves, and palm fronds often have brown jagged edges where the leaves have been chewed off. The topmost bud of a seedling palm is delicious, but is well protected by tough spikes. Elephants are passionately fond of the palm fruits and move from island to island in search of fruiting trees. Despite the palm's impressive height, an adult elephant can easily wrap its trunk round the stem and shake it vigorously to dislodge the fruits. Chacma baboons also like the sweet ginger-flavoured pith of *Hyphaene* fruits and often feed in the wake of elephants, collecting fruits that are shaken loose but not eaten.

Hyphaene fruits are the size of large apples, a tree, on average, bearing about 50 kilograms a year. The hard shiny brown shell covers a thin layer of edible flesh which encloses a bony kernel of vegetable 'ivory'. A baboon may carry a fruit a short distance, probably to prevent its being stolen by another baboon, but it is far too heavy to be carried by birds or small mammals. It is said that the *Hyphaene* seed must pass through the gut of an elephant to germinate. This is unlikely, though the seedling obviously benefits from starting life in a moist dung heap. The stimulus for germination is, in fact, fire, which is common on these islands in the dry season and, if uncontrolled, cause considerable damage.

Hyphaene palms generally withstand fire because the full diameter of their stem develops underground. The curious bulge mid-way down the grey fluted stem is a mystery. Research indicates that it is not related to water economy or strength. Nor does it prevent chacma baboons from shinning up and down the stems and robbing the fruits.

The tree's wide-based crown is one of the baboon's favourite nesting places. The dense crowns are used by other creatures, including buffalo weaver birds which build large communal nests there. When abandoned, the nests are taken over by tree rats. The palms are also used as roosts by bats. One of the great attractions of the crown is that the large fronds remain for a long time after they die, the dead leaves forming massive clusters that provide cover and shade.

In the heart of the sand islands, the vegetation becomes truly dry. The camelthorn acacia replaces the knobthorn, and the woodlands are interspersed with combretum and silver terminalia trees on very deep sands. Mopane woodlands grow where the soils contain more clay. Elephants love the roots of terminalia, but can feed only during the rains in the deep sand areas in which they grow.

These dry woodlands support the growth of sweet grasses, as well as tasty shrubs such as grewia (raisin berry) bushes with their nutritious leaves and abundance of small, brown and very sweet berries. The woodlands are populated by elephants, buffaloes, zebras, wildebeests, giraffes and kudus, especially in the rains when the trees have a flush of new leaves and the water pans are full. As the dry season advances and the pans dry out the animals gradually drift back to the floodplains where they are closer to water.

The onset of winter

Before the large animals return, the floodplains are relatively empty and interesting associations are at their most evident. Wattled cranes feed in shallow water, digging up roots of the grasses and sedges that lechwes also feed on. These large, elegant birds are the rarest of Africa's four crane species.

The Okavango Delta is one of the most important breeding grounds in the world for wattled cranes, which need large areas of undisturbed wetland to breed successfully. A pair of cranes requires roughly 30 hectares to nest and 150 hectares in which to feed. During their moult in spring cranes are particularly vulnerable to disturbance and predation. Non-breeding birds form highly nomadic flocks, travelling south to Makgadikgadi and beyond.

With the approach of winter the floodplains are dry and the ground hard, awaiting the floods. Chacma baboons and warthogs are solitary figures on the dusty plains. While warthogs are expert diggers, rooting up vegetation with their tusks on bended knees, male baboons are notoriously vigilant, defending their troop from predators. Warthogs tolerate the presence of baboons since they benefit from early warning of danger and baboons share the fruits of the warthogs' rooting and digging.

The low waters create unusually high concentrations of fish in the few shallow pools, attracting a frenzy of birds such as pelicans and marabou storks. The thin-faced bream is a predatory cichlid specialised for hunting in densely reeded areas, with a long thin body and snout. It lurks camouflaged behind reeds, protruding its jaws into a cone to suck in unwary fish. The climbing perch is another floodplains fish specialist. It has accessory breathing organs in the gills which enable it to live in the oxygen-deficient waters of shallow pools. When a pool is almost dry, a stranded climbing perch can move a short distance overland to a new pool by 'walking' on its side and pulling itself along with the serrated edge of its gill flap. How it determines the location of a nearby pool is a source of wonder.

In June winter sets in, bringing changes that in the Delta, where the presence of water tempers the cold and aridity, are more subtle than elsewhere in the Kalahari. At night, under cool clear skies laden with stars, buffaloes and lechwes move onto the islands to seek warmth beneath the big trees. On the islands nocturnal predators search for their much diminished prey. Snakes, frogs and musk shrews have gone into semi-hibernation, but tree rats still abound and are now the major prey of small carnivores. At night, little bee-eaters crowd together in narrow channels on slender reeds overhanging the water, huddled close to keep warm. Occasionally the entire line is disturbed as the end bird flies up and tries to squeeze into the cosy middle.

Mistletoe, snowdrops and winter grasses

Despite the cloudless skies, the chill of morning is burnt off only around noon. Life, both plant and animal, seems to have paused as if in suspense, waiting until warmth and rain bring renewed activity. There are no fruits or flowers on the trees, except for the delicate blossoms of the winter-flowering mistletoe which grows on knobthorn trees. They are a source of nectar for birds, carpenter bees, honey bees and ants in the dry season. The jewel colours of sunbirds – Marico's, white-bellied and collared – flash among the flowers.

Mistletoe berries are taken by birds such as pinkish crested barbets, which wipe the sticky seeds from their beaks onto the bark of trees, where some of them germinate. Acacias are generally the preferred host of the parasitic mistletoe as the dense thorny branches protect the plant from browsing animals.

The mistletoe is host to several caterpillar species, each with its own strategies for survival. The gregarious dotted border caterpillar depends on striking coloration and a hairy appearance to warn predators of its distastefulness. The larvae emerge together from the eggs, feed and move from leaf to leaf in a caravan. They also pupate together – all tactics for safety in numbers.

141

The caterpillar of the pretty short-barred sapphire butterfly mimics any portion of the mistletoe it happens to be feeding on. The larva is orange when it feeds on the flower and takes on a silvery-green coloration when it moves to a leaf, its head looking like the nibbled leaf edge. It pupates on the grey stem of the plant, where it resembles bird droppings. This type of protective mimicry means that the larva is safest alone.

The short-barred sapphire is a member of the lycaenid group of butterflies, highly specific to their food plant and with a fascinating lifecycle that makes use of those abundant little predators, ants. Most lycaenid caterpillars are 'milked' by ants, which rub a gland on the back of the larva to make it exude drops of honey-dew. In turn, the ants protect the larvae, sometimes taking them off their food plant and carrying them into the ant nest, safe from the ravages of grass fires and from birds and other predators. On emerging from their pupae, the butterflies make a quick exit from the nest as their wings expand.

In the winter lagoons the water is an icy blue, mirroring the immense cloudless skies. Water lily flowers have died back with the cold, and the papyrus stands tall and lifeless. In the glassy channels the only flowers are the delicate white blossoms of *Ottelia*, looking like snowdrops in an ice-covered meadow. The stems of this aquatic plant are covered with spiky bumps and a thin layer of mucus, which help deter fish from eating them. The fragile blossoms are supported on a single air bladder that keeps them above water for pollination. This is a lean time for aquatic predators as the Delta's waters are too cold for fish to breed.

On the floodplains the winter grasses are dry and coarse, but the large mammals gradually return from the dry interior of the Kalahari to congregate there. The large predators arrive in their wake – for them this is a season of plenty. The first animals to arrive are the most water-dependent herbivores.

A grazing order exists in which animals such as buffaloes and zebras (which can tolerate the coarsest vegetation) feed on the tallest and least palatable floodplain grasses, making shorter, more nutritious, grasses available to selective feeders such as sables, wildebeests and tsessebes. These graze the grass to the length preferred by steenboks, impalas and warthogs. In this way a large number and variety of grazing animals can co-exist without competition.

There is an air of expectancy on the dry brown floodplains in the depths of the cold, rainless winter. An amazing event is awaited, which will bring new life to the Delta's southerly grasslands . . . the floods are coming from the north.

CHAPTER NINE

Flood-tide

Pula, the word for rain in Botswana, is also the name of the nation's currency – such is the value placed on this precious resource. The rains fall mainly in the hot season, from November to March, but the pattern constantly changes; in some years there is almost no rain and drought prevails. The build-up to rain lasts for months, large continental air masses bringing with them high atmospheric pressure. Dark skies, high winds and heavy heat – the high-pressure heat that comes from being in the heart of a massive continent – produce nothing but storms of sand.

Massive cumulus clouds and isolated showers characterise the Delta's rains. Size is deceptive. An isolated storm that appears small in the vastness of the Delta may be a hundred kilometres wide. There is immense power in the blackness of the storm clouds. The heavy atmosphere builds slowly. Clouds, distant at first, race across the sky, a gun-metal grey with leading edges tinged gold by the rays of a sun that will soon be obliterated. The wind howls and swirls; the tall grass crackles, rustles and whispers in the hot air that swirls beneath the darkening sky.

In the far distance another isolated storm moves across the horizon. The clouds now fill the sky; lightning flashes and thunder rumbles in their purple heart. The rain in the distance is white. Leaves are torn from the trees and carried high by winds that continue to gain momentum. White egrets shimmer against the slate-grey clouds, the birds tossed about with the leaves. Suddenly there is a lull, and rain falls. When the clouds move the rain-washed landscape receives the sun's rays making a rainbow in the sky. Before long the air is hot again.

The Delta always has more rain than other parts of the Kalahari, its water and vegetation no doubt creating their own local climate, much as tropical forests do. The rains raise the level of water and although they provide a third of the Delta's water, 95 per cent of it is lost through evaporation. Their impact, meanwhile, is small in comparison with another rain-borne event – the annual floods.

In the highlands of Angola the rains begin in November. Rainwater collects within this huge catchment and is channelled down the Cuito and Cubango rivers and thence to the Okavango, swelling the river's banks and producing a flood-tide of water that travels southwards. In the upper reaches of the Delta the river reaches peak height in February and the Panhandle, thus, is the only area to receive the floods at the same time as the rains.

Flood waters

As the flood travels down the Okavango River, the river overflows its banks, inundating the land and covering the sandbanks. On reaching the fan-shaped Delta the water spreads, flowing over river banks between clumps of reeds and papyrus, covering floodplains and slowly raising the water level in lagoons and backwaters.

The flood's front moves slowly, travelling at speeds that rarely exceed a kilometre a day – partly because of the flatness of the terrain and partly because the water is slowed by swamp vegetation. At this speed the floods take some five months to travel the length of the Delta, replenishing life in the southern floodplains in the midst of the dry season.

The papyrus swamps in the Panhandle are now flushed with fresh water, bringing dramatic change. Sitatungas calve and move out into the previously inaccessible swamplands where there is more food and cover. African skimmer chicks have already fledged and, as the rising water slowly covers the sandbanks, the last few skimmers leave their summer breeding grounds to travel north, not returning to grace the sunset waters of the Okavango River until the following

September. Crocodiles' eggs also hatch and the young crocodiles find food and safety in new pools in the swamplands beyond the main river.

Packs of hunting barbels that have swum northwards find breeding grounds in the shallow floodplains. There seems to be an urgency to spawn at the start of the floods – in water so shallow that the fish can barely swim – perhaps to guarantee a current that flushes and oxygenates the eggs. Fishermen wade into the shallows in the Panhandle to spear barbels as they spawn.

In the swamps and reedbeds of the Okavango the seasonal floods displace the 'old water', which is enriched with the organic matter, sludge and detritus that has accumulated in the swamps between floods. In this way the flood regime has an impact throughout the Delta, enriching the lower regions with regular supplies of silt and detritus as well as providing water to sustain the seasonal swamps and floodplains. Slowly the floodwaters filter and trickle through endless reedbeds, raising the level of water around sand islands and leaving, after evaporation, salt deposits on the sandy surface.

In the northern seasonal swamps and lagoons the water level rises slowly, almost imperceptibly. The floods bring with them many subtle changes. Coiled lily stems untwist to compensate for the increase in the water's depth. The burrows of semi-aquatic rodents and shrews are flooded by the rising waters and have to be evacuated. The floods arrive here towards the

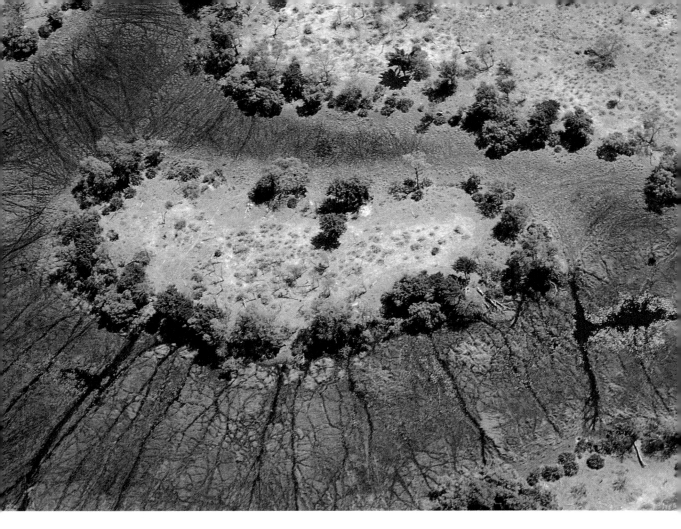

Termite mounds, pictured here on an Okavango island (opposite), dominate the landscape. At night the rusty spotted genet (this page, top) waits in ambush in a tree, while the semi-aquatic marsh mongoose (bottom) forages along the edges of islands.
OVERLEAF: *Large areas of grassland are flooded each year.*

Impalas are both browsers and grazers, and are abundant in the transitional habitat between grasslands and woodlands fringing the islands and land masses of the Okavango Delta.

The semi-aquatic red lechwe (this page, top) usually runs through shallow water to escape potential predators. Red lechwes and chacma baboons (bottom) are the most numerous mammals in the Delta. In the dry season, Cape buffaloes concentrate in large herds on the floodplains (opposite).

New grasses sprout from flooded winter grasslands (this page, top). The winter-flowering mistletoe (bottom right) is browsed by the dotted border caterpillar (bottom left), which feeds and pupates in numbers as a tactic against predation. On winter nights, little bee-eaters huddle together for warmth (opposite).

In the cold dry season elephants return from the Kalahari interior to the waters of the north and west (below), and hippos (opposite top) bask after the winter chill of early morning. The palm islands of the Lower Delta (opposite bottom), reminiscent of Makgadikgadi's palm belt, are isolated by the floods.

The wild dog (opposite) comes to the flooded grasslands in search of prey. Wild dogs are highly social, living and hunting in packs, males remaining in their pack of birth while females over two years of age join unrelated packs. Africa's largest stork, the saddle-bill (this page, top and bottom), flies to floodplain grasslands to feed on fish brought in by the flood.

end of the hot summer. By flushing out the back-water swamps they revitalise the waters and provide additional habitats for cichlid fingerlings which have been raised in the shallow back-waters in summer.

The breeding and movements of many fish species are adapted to the floods. The tide trav-elling down the main channels is a signal to tiger fish, which travel upstream to spawn. The exact location of their spawning grounds in the Delta, possibly the secluded reedy Jao 'flats' of the Upper Delta, is a mystery. After spawning they return to overwinter in the deeper lagoons.

Peat mats

Organic matter and detritus brought down with the floods contributes to the formation of float-ing 'peat mats' which play their part in the Delta's constantly changing waterways. As the floodwaters pass through backwater lagoons they slow down and deposit their load of detri-tus which, together with the mass of decaying vegetation on the bottom of the lagoon, forms a fibrous layer. This is the start of a peat mat that gains form and bulk with the establishment of various aquatic plants such as water lilies, water chestnuts and bladderworts.

During the warm summer months micro-organisms living in the mat produce methane gases which cause the mat to float to the water's surface. Here aquatic plants can grow and flower. Approaching winter cold inhibits the activity of the micro-organisms and the mats sink again.

This cycle of wetting and drying eventually stabilises peat mats so that they no longer sink and vegetation, in particular coarse miscanthus swamp grass, becomes well established.

Peat mats are used by many swamp crea-tures. Swamp worms colonise these floating mats. Like earthworms, they consume vast quan-tities of organic matter and mud which are then cast onto the surface of the mat. In this way swamp worms play an important role in break-ing down plant material and making nutrients and oxygen available to other organisms that inhabit the mats. To cope with low-oxygen con-ditions the swamp worm protrudes its hind end above the mud and folds it over to trap a bub-ble of air, which it pulls back into its burrow.

Darters perch on mats to dry their wings after fishing, and small crocodiles bask on them in the sun. Jacanas frequently land on the mats, where they peck bloodworms from lily buds and forage for worms in the mud. In time several peat mats join to create larger and larger areas, which are colonised by miscanthus grass, result-ing in extensive regions of peat bog.

These grass clumps may grow large enough to block the flow of water in places and, in time, dry out. Permanent beds of grass develop where there used to be water. The final stage to the for-mation of dry land, which may take decades, is the metamorphosis of peat as a result of smoul-dering underground fires fed by natural gases. This leaves bare earth which is colonised by dry-land grass, forming floodplain grasslands.

Fires and changing waterways

River channels filling with sediments and drying as the waters seek another course also cause the Delta's smouldering peat fires. As the slowing current drops its load of sand, it raises the bed of the channel until its water runs elsewhere. Reedbeds on either side of the abandoned channel, which grow on a thick bed of peat, dry out and ignite from methane gases deep within the peat.

Nutrients released by fires promote the growth of grasses on the newly formed floodplains. The raised beds of former river channels remain as chains of sandy islands, flanked by grassland. Pools of water may remain, creating an ideal habitat for larger mammals such as buffaloes and lechwes, which now have new pastures interspersed with permanent water.

Even major channels in the Okavango are thought to have a life of less than a hundred years. The death of a watercourse can occur when water is slowed by blockages of vegetation and lost to newly formed drainage systems. Free-floating islands of fast-growing papyrus also play a role; it is not long before a small 'plug' of vegetation grows into a large dam. Abandoned dugouts, the traditional river craft of fishermen, may also be a cause of blockage.

Elephant activity can change the pattern of water flow, especially in phragmites reedbeds. Elephants are among the few creatures that can feed on this tall, bamboo-like grass. Towards the end of the dry season, these largest of land mammals wade into lagoons, churning up reeds as they dig for the tasty roots; soon the elephants are covered in mud and the reedbeds are flattened. New channels open for water to pass through and chunks of reeds may float off and block other, smaller, channels. The regular movement of hippos from water to dry land is another major factor in creating and maintaining channels in the Delta.

So dynamic are the Okavango's waterways that small changes may occur in as little as a year; others are more gradual. At the turn of the last century there was a major shift in flow from the Thaoge River, which used to flow into Lake Ngami, to the eastern Ngokha and Mborogha systems. This has led to the drying of Lake Ngami and the western edge of the Okavango Delta. When the British explorers Livingstone and Oswald visited Lake Ngami in the mid 1800s the lake was some 100 kilometres in circumference. It began to dry in the 1870s and today is usually dry. The drying Thaoge River may never reach the lake again.

In the last two decades there has been a change in flow eastwards from the Mborogha River to the Moanatshira. More recently – and on a shorter time scale – the pattern of waterways around the south-west of Chief's Island has altered. Such changes create a mosaic of different habitats and maintain diversity.

Changing waterways are not the only agents of transformation in the Okavango. Surface fires are common; three-quarters of the reedbeds

162

are burnt at some time during the year. Papyrus fires are often started by lightning from summer storms, but more often by hunters who wish to reduce plant cover and improve visibility when hunting antelopes attracted to the flush of green shoots that grow after a fire.

Papyrus may look unburnable, but its high phenol content makes it highly combustible. Once papyrus has caught fire it burns fiercely. The feathery tops fizzle and pop like firecrackers as, fuelled by hot air, the flames race through the reedbeds until they reach the edge of a channel and are extinguished by the water. However, in low water thousands of hectares are destroyed. The high incidence of uncontrolled fires in the Okavango is very damaging to the environment.

Birds, including yellow-billed kites and marsh harriers, are attracted to insects disturbed by the flames. After a fire, open-billed storks congregate in numbers on the charred stubby reedbeds to pick off mussels and snails. From October to December, when carmine bee-eaters are forming their breeding colonies, fires attract large numbers of these beautiful crimson birds. The blue-cheeked bee-eater, a winter migrant from the Middle East, hunts over papyrus fires, catching dragonflies with a spectacular 'back-flip': it glides fast under its prey and momentarily arches its back and head to snatch the insect.

Flooding in the Lower Delta

The area covered by water doubles in the northern perennial swamps during the floods, but increases tenfold as it spills out over the floodplains of the Lower Delta. The arrival of the floods in the southern dry floodplains is a dramatic event. Its scale is best appreciated from the air at twilight, when the Delta can be seen stretching over the horizon, the dark shapes of sand islands and the dusky-gold floodplains surrounded by fingers of floodwater shimmering like threads of mercury in the sun's dying rays.

The first sign of the water's arrival in the southern plains is a small trickle along a dry watercourse or well-worn hippo path. Soon the trickle becomes a strong flow, forcing grasses and insects from its path. Within a day the narrow channel has overflowed and blue water spreads out through tawny grasses and covers the parched earth.

Its effect on plant and animal life is immediate. Stranded ants and grasshoppers scramble up those grass stems that remain above water and are quickly taken by small fish travelling with the flood-tide. Birds congregate on the floodplains, picking up insects escaping from the flood. Bennett's woodpecker – unusual in that it forages mostly on the ground – is quick to take advantage of the water's arrival, probing with its tongue in the wet mud at the water's edge. The floodwater is enriched as it sweeps over the plains, picking up nutrients from termite nests, insects, grasses, seeds, animal dung and other sources.

Aquatic creatures also take advantage of these conditions. Tiny cichlid fish nibble the submerged droppings of floodplain animals. The shallows are not deep enough for tiger fish, but African pike, the Okavango's other dominant fish predator, follow small fish there. Pike and tiger fish are closely related and this separation of habitat helps prevent competition. Pike need the cover of dense reeds to hunt, ambushing their prey and striking out suddenly with a sideways swipe. Cichlid fish spawn in summer warmth regardless of floods, but more hardy fish, such as climbing perch and many catfish species, avail themselves of the new waters to reproduce.

Pike breed in the watery grasslands and reedbeds soon after the floods arrive. They lay their eggs on a 'nest' of foam that the adult pair builds at the start of breeding on the water's surface, well placed in a dense cover of sheltered reeds to help the nest keep its shape. Pike have an extra 'skin flap' on the side of the mouth, which can be used to blow foam bubbles. The female spawns beneath the nest and numerous eggs float upwards to become enveloped in the foam. This is a good breeding strategy in swampy habitats to prevent eggs from falling onto the sludgy bottom where they would die in the low-oxygen environment.

The eggs hatch after a few days and the young fish remain attached to the foam by thin adhesive threads while they live off the remains of the egg yolk. After several days the yolk is exhausted and the small fish become independent. The adult pike guard the nest and replenish the foam until the young fish are big enough to leave the nest and catch and eat small insects such as mosquito larvae. They develop into fierce little predators that can take prey the same size as themselves – sometimes their own siblings.

In the mists of a winter's morning, large swarms of mayflies collect over the water's surface in graceful aerial dances. The swarms are generally all male since males immediately seize females and fly away with them to mate. The female lays her eggs on the water, where they sink to the bottom and hatch into nymphs. Adult mayflies die a few days after mating and egg-laying; conversely the nymphs take a year, and sometimes more, to develop.

The change from nymph to adult mayfly is a wonder of nature. After passing through 23 moults during its underwater life, the nymph rises to the surface. Here, supported by surface tension, its casing splits and the winged 'pro-adult' emerges. Flitting to a reed, it moults once more into its adult form, the only insect in the world known to moult after the wings are functional.

Emergent mayflies are taken by fish, birds and bats. Some are caught in the gossamer threads of the webs of orb-web spiders in tall reeds. The advancing floodwaters bring with them thousands of floating mayflies that have died after their brief adult lives. They accumulate at small blockages and along the edges of the flood, where they are picked out by jacanas and other birds.

As the floodplains are submerged the vegetation changes. Delicate pink storm lilies, whose bulbs have remained dormant in the grasslands for a year, brighten the land. Snow lilies, sedges and other aquatic plants grow among the submerged grasses, which together with flooded animal dung and drowned insects provide food for various creatures.

Fish in the shallow waters are easy pickings for birds, which use different fishing methods to secure their prey. The pied kingfisher hovers for dozens of wing-beats before it plummets into the water; enormous saddle-billed storks stalk ponderously, their eyes focused on the water's surface as they search for a movement they can stab at with their long bills; the hamerkop stirs the mud with its feet so as to disturb its favourite prey, the platanna frog.

The flush of succulent green vegetation attracts lechwes into the water to graze. Waterbuck are much less numerous in the Okavango than their close relative, the red lechwe, being less well adapted to feeding on low-quality vegetation. In front of the flood the earth is softened by the rising water table and here warthogs dig and wallow, covering their skins with cooling mud to keep away irritating biting flies. Spurwing and Egyptian geese arrive in large flocks and wander along the shoreline, picking at green shoots.

The floods push larger animals back to the fringes and interiors of the autumn woods. They emerge to drink from the fresh water that runs in rivers instead of stagnating in pools. Sable antelopes leave the mopane woods at midday to drink, watching for predators. Zebras and giraffes water in the late afternoon, their coats a perfect foil to the grey bark and russet-gold leaves of mopane trees. At dusk herds of elephants emerge from the shade, scuffing holes on the edges of the flood with their feet to create pools deep enough to drink from.

Predators, too, come to the drowning grasslands. Larger carnivores, such as spotted hyaenas, lions and hunting dogs, wade through the shallow water in search of prey. The speedy, pack-hunting wild dog seldom makes a kill in water. However, spotted hyaenas may run their exhausted and frightened prey there to slow them down. Vultures spiral over the kills, and the Bateleur eagle soars in lazy circles. Huge herds of zebras and wildebeests, which have roamed the interior for most of the year, return to the Delta, as though the scent of the coming flood has drawn them in.

Journey's end

After a journey that has taken many months the last of the Okavango's waters are lost in the shallow floodplains of the Lower Delta – sucked by parched sands, burnt off by the sun and used by innumerable plants and animals.

The journey does not quite end here. The lower channels and waterways of the Delta meet a barrier, the Thamalakane Fault, the waters turning abruptly to flow south-east in a single straight channel. Buried beneath several hundred metres of sand, the only evidence of the fault is the river's sudden change in direction.

It takes with it the last of the Delta's water, a fraction of the flow that arrived in the Panhandle from the Angolan highlands. The Thamalakane River becomes the Boteti River, which carries the Okavango's waters several hundred kilometres into the Kalahari in a river valley too wide and deep to be made by such a meagre flow – a reminder of the size of the great river that used to flow into Lake Makgadikgadi.

For millennia the wildlife of the region has retreated to the Boteti when drought lingered too long. Even now the animals that inhabit the Makgadikgadi pans and the interior grasslands come here in the dry season. Today the water is in even shorter supply. There is too much competition from cattle, people and the Orapa diamond mine at the end of the river. A hundred years ago David Livingstone wrote of hunting sitatungas at Lake Xau – evidence of an impressive lake that was fed by the Boteti. Xau now stands dry and desolate, peppered by the skeletons of animals that reached their traditional watering point and, finding it dry, were too weak to go further.

In a very high flood the flood waters might reach the edges of the Makgadikgadi before they are burnt off in the salt pans in the swirling heat. More often, however, the last of the Okavango's waters end in a muddy pool, dwarfed by the wide banks of the Boteti.

CHAPTER TEN

Land of the Hunter

deep in the sandveldt a small cluster of grass-thatched huts indicates the presence of man. A band of honey-coloured people, lightly clad in skins and beads, set about their daily tasks. Women and children wander into the wilderness with digging sticks and leather bags. Before the day is through they will have returned with a feast – truffles dug from the earth, tsama melons, sun-dried brown berries with the sweetness of raisins, nuts and pods, tasty roots and starchy tubers – the harvest of the Kalahari.

The men are out at dawn, after an evening of preparation, spreading poison on their arrow-heads and telling stories of past hunts. Lightly and swiftly they step through the sand, looking for tracks, keeping in contact with each other with soft, bird-like calls. From the faint signs in the sand they can tell which species has passed, what sex and age, at what time and what the animal was doing. The quarry is stalked and shot, and then tracked while the poison takes effect. By dusk the meat is taken home. There is dancing and singing that night under the Milky Way, which Bushmen call the 'backbone of the sky'.

Bushmen are the oldest of Africa's peoples and the earliest race to live in the Kalahari. Never in the history of Africa has a people lived for so long on a land without changing or destroying it. Hunter-gatherers, they did not consider it necessary to grow crops or keep livestock when nature provided. Tragically, this sensitive race continues to be persecuted and marginalised. Very few Bushmen remain today, living as their ancestors did.

At one time Bushmen occupied most of Africa but they gradually lost ground to more ambitious and aggressive races. The Kalahari became one of their last hunting grounds. Their much-publicised eviction in relatively recent times from their traditional lands in the Central Kalahari Game Reserve – a policy for which the reasons are still unclear – is regarded by many as a tragic injustice, clouding Botswana's otherwise well-respected democracy.

Bushman legends suggest that once, long ago, they lived in a much lusher place. In the beginning, when the earth was covered with water, the legendary Bushman hero, the Mantis, was carried over the waters by the wise bee. The bee became weary in his search for dry land, flying lower and lower as the weight of the Mantis dragged him down. Finally, as he sank he suddenly saw a great white flower, the night lily perhaps, half-open in the darkness. The exhausted bee laid the Mantis in the heart of the flower and died. As the sun's rays warmed the flower, the Mantis awoke and from this seed the first Bushman was born.

A hunter's code

Of the 262 animal species known to the !Kung people of the western Kalahari, it has been found that only 80 are hunted. While hunting is important for food and is of social significance, killing merely for sport is unknown. A few species are taboo. Elephants, for example, are not hunted as they are considered to have the intelligence of man. Ostriches are seldom killed – they run too fast – but their eggs are prized for food and for making ornaments. Hunting large animals, such as antelopes and giraffes, is the work of young men, using poisoned arrows.

The hunting code of Bushmen is based on social values rather than material gain. A hunter must remain modest about his kills so as not to create envy. If he has had a series of successful hunts, he stops hunting for a while to give other hunters a chance to excel.

The way poison is obtained for arrowheads illustrates well their makers' understanding and use of the environment. Toxin is taken from pupae of the flea-beetle, the two most poison-ous species of which feed on the leaves of commiphora bushes. Hunters dig deep into the sand around bushes to collect the pupae. They roll the pupa between their fingers to soften it and spread the orange body fluid directly over the arrow's tip or mix it with acacia gum and saliva to make it extra-adhesive.

Bracelets of the morning

To the west of the Delta, three granite outcrops rise from the flatness of the vast sandy expanses. People have lived around the Tsodilo Hills for thousands of years. Hundreds of rock paintings tell their story. Most are painted on west-facing slopes that catch the afternoon sun or on concave rocks on bluffs that overlook the Kalahari. Each site seems as carefully chosen as the theme of the painting itself. Wild animals dominate, expertly executed in ochre colours, rhinos prominent among them.

One lively painting in the hills is of a grotto of naked men dancing with erect penises; the few men without are in a healing trance. The scene is believed to depict the Eland Dance, performed to cure a person of ailments of the feet. The Gemsbok Dance is performed for ailments of the heart, and the Giraffe Dance for those of the head. Traditional Bushmen still name illnesses after animals, each called on to cure particular ailments.

The !Kung call the hills 'the bracelets of the morning'. Indeed, the sun's morning rays touch one faceted rock face and then another, giving

To the west of the Delta's Panhandle, three granite outcrops (top) rise from the flat Kalahari sands. The Tsodilo Hills (bottom), called the 'bracelets of morning' by the !Kung Bushmen, have been inhabited by humans for several thousand years.

Most of the rock paintings (top right and left) on the rock faces of Tsodilo depict wild animals, and attest to the continued importance of hunting to the people who lived there. Nature's art is evident on rock faces covered by colourful lichens (bottom).

The traditional Bushman dress of skins and beads is being replaced by western style clothing, but some women still wear their colourful beads (below). The old hunter and his son (opposite bottom) illustrate the merging of old ways and new. In the Delta some BaYei women still fish using their traditional baskets (opposite top).

Baskets (opposite top and bottom) are woven by women from the young leaves of Hyphaene *palms. The fine quality of this traditional craft is making Botswana baskets a thriving industry. At a cattle post (opposite), Herero women walk past, their petticoats and bonnets a legacy perhaps from the German occupation of their former home, Namibia.*

Too many animals in one place for too long results in overgrazing (opposite top). Increasingly, wild animals die of starvation (opposite bottom) as a result of competition with cattle for food. Fences were built to control the spread of foot-and-mouth disease in cattle: the Buffalo Fence around the Delta (this page, top) and the Makalamabedi Fence beyond the Boteti River (bottom).

*The need for cattle to drink daily (this page, bottom) creates problems as cattle posts (top)
penetrate the Kalahari – formerly the domain of mobile and light-footed animals.
Wetland meets desert (opposite), the Okavango's waters spilling and spreading
out over Botswana's Kalahari sands.*

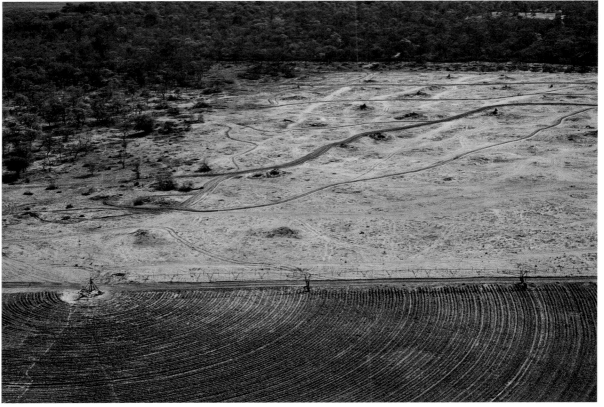

Large areas of the Delta have been sprayed (this page, top and bottom) to control tsetse flies, which transmit a deadly parasite, but no one knows what effect such chemicals have on wildlife. Fires, often started by man, burn over 70 per cent of the Delta each year (opposite top), causing great damage. Irrigated farming (opposite bottom) will help Botswana increase its food production.

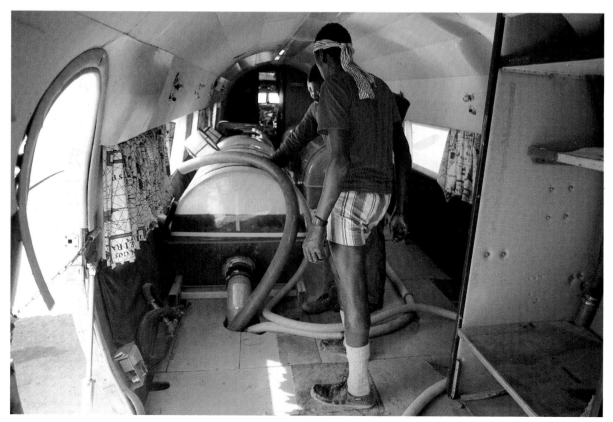

Salvinia (inset) is an exotic weed that quickly infests African waters, choking aquatic life and blocking waterways. An outbreak in the Lower Delta in 1986, presumably brought in from the Kwando and Linyanti swamps, covered Xini Lagoon within weeks.

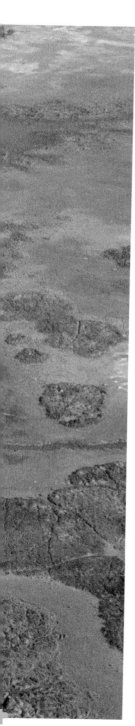

Hippos (top) also contribute to the dispersal of the salvinia weed, and so a fence (bottom) was built around Xini Lagoon to restrict their movement further into the Delta. The outbreak was controlled by pumping the lagoon dry, but the possibility of other outbreaks in the Delta will always be of concern.

the hills texture and warmth. Filtered sunbeams fall between clefts, picking out colours in the rocks – sandstone yellows washed with pinks. Granite stone faces are patterned with lime-green, white and orange lichens. Sandy paths weave through the hills beneath trees whose leaves catch the light as they stir in the breeze. There is magic in these sacred hills.

Nearly every bush and tree has a use, but mongongo trees, which grow in shady groves in deep Kalahari sands, are the most cherished. The outer flesh of the fruit is edible and encloses a nutritious, almond-flavoured nut. Rainwater collects in the trunks of older trees, providing gatherers with water on long foraging trips. Each mongongo grove is individually known and owned but the nuts are freely shared in the spirit of the Bushman way of life. The landscape of Tsodilo has changed little over the centuries, and fruit-bearing trees such as marulas and mongongos, grewia bushes, acacias and shepherd's trees still grace the rocky valleys. Sadly, some paintings have now been scarred by graffiti.

The peopling of Botswana

The Bushmen did not live in isolation from outside influences. Archaeological finds, particularly in the Tsodilo Hills, show that Bantu pastoralists and traders also inhabited the area since at least AD 500. Cattle occurred there as early as the third century AD. Their remains have been found along with those of zebras, wildebeests, warthogs and other wild animals. Sea shells indicate there was trade with the Atlantic, and fish remains are evidence of local trade with people of the Delta.

The Delta was first inhabited by Bushmen, who made fishing nets from the fibres of aloe and sanserveria, and would sometimes poison fish in pools by throwing in the bark of the motsebe (croton) tree. They fished in lagoons from water rafts made of papyrus, their penetration of the Delta restricted by the nature of their rafts until the BaYei people introduced dug-outs.

With the arrival of Bantu peoples the importance of cattle for the first time superceded that of wildlife. The BaTswana, Bantu pastoralists from the south, established dominance in the region, bringing with them an organised political system that included a monarchy and courts and laws, along with social ranking based on birthright and wealth through ownership of cattle. Despite infighting and splitting of sub-groups, they have retained sovereignty in what is now Botswana.

By the eighteenth century Bushmen and BaKgalagadi, an ethnic group similar to the BaTswana, were driven west into the Kalahari or became servants to the BaTswana in the area. Rich and powerful in comparison with hunter/gatherer groups, the BaTswana bought tobacco from eastern tribes and traded with the BaKgalagadi for skins, which they made into karosses and exchanged in the south for cattle.

Although the life of the BaTswana peoples centred on cattle, wildlife remained for them an important source of food. Two or three regiments, each composed of young men of a certain age, would go out on hunts, known as 'letsholo'. In the winter they travelled long distances, sometimes journeying a thousand kilometres to the rich hunting grounds of the north. The meat from a season's hunting was dried and brought back to the villages.

In the eighteenth and nineteenth centuries other groups arrived to make their home in the Kalahari. The expansion of the Lozi State in north-western Zambia in the 1750s caused the BaYei to migrate southwards from their homes along the Zambezi River. At that time the HaMbukushu were living around the Tsodilo Hills. According to one of their legends, they were let down from heaven onto the hills by their creator, Nyambi, leaving imprints on the rocks.

The BaYei and HaMbukushu were pastoralists as well as hunters. Moving through areas of tsetse fly, they left behind their stock, relying instead on hunting and fishing. The BaYei journeyed south on wooden dug-outs (mokoros) through the Selinda Spillway and into the Delta's complex waterways. With the drying-up of the Selinda and Savuti channels this journey is now impossible.

In the mid-nineteenth century a new type of hunter entered the scene. Until then the ivory resources of the country were virtually untouched. Stories of cattle kraals built of ivory tusks lured commercial hunters who made huge profits from such wildlife resources. Their arrival with their ox-wagons and guns brought great changes. Large-scale hunting resulted in the indiscriminate and widespread killing of wildlife, and records from as early as 1888 ascribe the depletion of wildlife to the use of guns. The BaTswana acted as middlemen between traders and hunter-gatherers, thereby building up their own wealth and power and transforming the flexible relations that had hitherto existed between various groups.

Among the last to settle in Botswana were the Herero, who came to southern Africa from the lakes of central Africa around the sixteenth century. In 1884 South West Africa was declared a German colony and by the turn of the century the colonists had turned on the Herero, planning to disarm them and take their cattle in lieu of debts and taxes. In 1904 the Herero, faced with a campaign of mass killing, fled to join relatives who had settled in northern Botswana. In their flight they lost their cattle, and had to start a new life as servants to the few established Herero who owned cattle. Expert in cattle management, however, they built up their own herds, thus reaching economic independence relatively quickly. Many Herero returned home when Namibia gained independence in 1998.

Cattle versus wildlife

Permanent villages and cattle posts were established near permanent water in the Kalahari by pastoralists, who moved their livestock deep into the sandveldt during the rains. Since they preferred to save their cattle – a form of currency and a source of wealth – they continued to hunt. But the teeming wildlife of the Kalahari was not an inexhaustible resource. Commercial hunting with guns and the expansion of cattle farming began to reduce the vast herds, but it was only in the last 50 years that the rapid and large-scale expansion of Botswana's cattle industry impacted severely on grasslands and wildlife.

This expansion began in the 1950s, when modern technology made it possible to drill deep boreholes. For the first time man and cattle could occupy the waterless regions of the Kalahari. For thousands of years such areas had been inhabited only by wild animals, delicately built, light of foot and highly mobile. Now cattle, heavy-hooved and dependent on water, walked daily to the same watering point, restricted to a small range that soon became heavily grazed. A widening circle of naked sand began to spread around each borehole, the patchwork extending as more boreholes were sunk.

Cattle began to have a far-reaching impact on wildlife – through loss of range and disruption of animal movement by fences. These were border fences that separated Botswana from neighbouring Namibia and South Africa, fences along major roads and a vast network of veterinary cordon fences. Veterinary fences are designed to control the spread of foot-and-mouth disease, a contagious disease that occurs in buffalo and in African cattle without causing major harm. It is much feared, however, by commercial farmers as the disease can spread like wildfire and infected livestock and meat must be destroyed.

Most of Botswana's fences were built to comply with strict European Union (EU) beef import regulations, which stipulate that cattle must be free of foot-and-mouth disease (Botswana receives 25 per cent more than the world market price for beef from Europe). The EU agreement with Botswana, known as the Lome Convention, has been steadily renewed and is scheduled for renegotiation in 2005. In its wake the national cattle herd increased from 1 million to 3.5 million head in just over a decade A network of fences separates and quarantines cattle from wildlife in the north, where they could have contact with buffaloes, which are possible carriers of the disease. The fences act like long drift nets through a sea of bush.

Fences, fences everywhere

Thousands of kilometres of fences now carve up much of Botswana, a network which has been extended around the Okavango region. Until recently, veterinary fences were built without environmental impact assessments. Criss-crossing vast areas of wilderness, they fragment habitat and impede the movement of wildlife in search of forage and water. The Kuke Fence erected in 1958 caused the loss of 95 per cent of the central Kalahari's wildebeest population in the early 1980s and ranks among the great conservation tragedies of southern Africa.

The Kuke Fence marks the northern boundary of the disease-free beef export zone. It stretches for 300 kilometres across the Kalahari,

VETERINARY CORDON FENCES

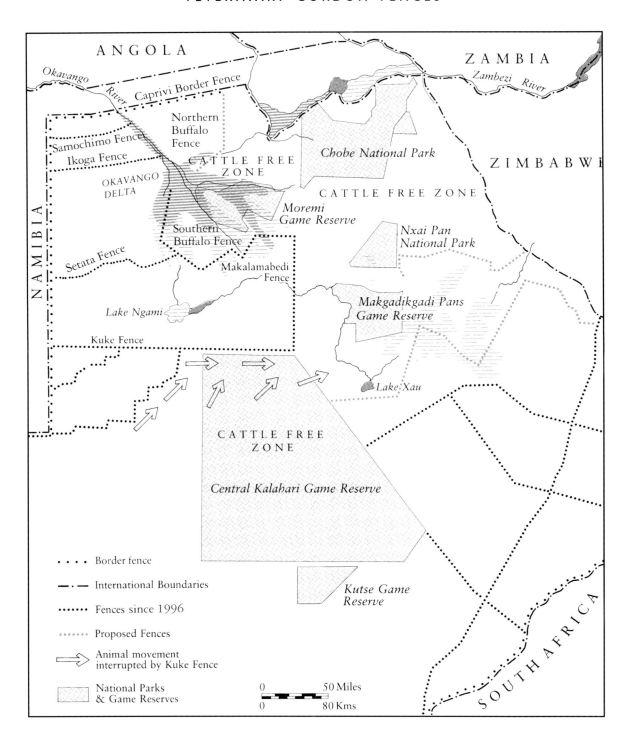

ANGOLA

Okavango

River

Caprivi Border Fence

ZAMBIA

Zambezi River

NAMIBIA

Samochimo Fence

Ikoga Fence

Northern
Buffalo
Fence

CATTLE FREE
ZONE

Chobe National Park

ZIMBABWE

OKAVANGO
DELTA

Moremi
Game Reserve

CATTLE FREE ZONE

Southern
Buffalo Fence

Nxai Pan
National Park

Setata Fence

Makalamabedi
Fence

Lake Ngami

Makgadikgadi Pans
Game Reserve

Kuke Fence

Lake Xau

CATTLE FREE
ZONE

Central Kalahari Game Reserve

Kutse Game
Reserve

SOUTH AFRICA

· · · ·   Border fence

— · — ·   International Boundaries

· · · · · ·   Fences since 1996

· · · · · · ·   Proposed Fences

⇒   Animal movement
interrupted by Kuke Fence

National Parks
& Game Reserves

0   50 Miles

0   80 Kms

almost dividing Botswana in half and separating the animals of the waterless central Kalahari from the great water crescent of the north. In the past, these well-watered areas were always available to animals in times of drought, enabling a large proportion of animals to survive until conditions improved.

Interestingly, the Buffalo Fence, built around the south-eastern perimeter of the Delta to separate buffaloes from cattle, is an example of a useful fence. As it confines wild animals to the wetland, it does not interrupt their movement to water. Furthermore it acts as a barrier between the wilderness and the increasing number of people and cattle outside of the fence.

In the drought years of the 1980s thousands of hartebeests died along fences in the west of the country. Herds of wildebeests that once more migrated northwards reached the Kuke Fence and were channelled to Lake Xau, which was dry and over-grazed. An estimated 50 000 of the 80 000 that arrived at Lake Xau in 1983 died there. In 1986, there was no migration; the population had crashed. Aerial surveys in 1987 counted only 260 wildebeests in the central Kalahari. An estimated 300 000 wildebeests, 260 000 hartebeests and 60 000 zebras died.

The Okavango region itself remained unfenced until relatively recently. Unexpectedly, in 1995, a virulent cattle disease known as Contagious Bovine Pleuro Pneumonia (CBPP) broke out along the northern Botswana border. It is thought to have come from infected cattle

from Namibia. The Botswana government acted quickly to stop its spread by building a series of parallel fences (the Samochima, Ikoga and Setata fences) from the western edge of the Delta to the Namibian border. Farmers, who feared their infected cattle would be exterminated, sneaked them around the quarantine fences.

The Kuke Fence was the last barrier against spread of the disease. To stop the disease spreading to the export cattle to the south, it was decided that the entire herd of 360 000 Ngamiland cattle north of the fence be exterminated. The exercise was carried out swiftly, with police and military assistance to maintain quarantine measures. The outbreak was finally brought under control in May 1997.

To seal off the entire Namibian Caprivi border and prevent cattle moving into Botswana a major, double electric fence was built. The extension of the Northern Buffalo Fence to the border fence isolated a large section of land to the east of the Panhandle. Conservationists, in particular CI and WWF, protested at this dramatic proliferation of fences and the blocking of an important wildlife corridor.

CI became part of a new committee, the Ad Hoc Committee on Fences, comprised of members of Botswana's Department of Animal Health, Department of Wildlife, National Conservation Strategy Agency and key conservation groups. For the first time, officials from different arms of government combined with conservation groups to discuss the thorny issue of the impact of cattle fences and possible mitigation measures. The government agreed to the committee's recommendation that a 40-kilometre stretch of the Caprivi Border Fence be removed where it reaches the Kwando River, thereby opening up a small but important wildlife corridor.

This was the first time in Botswana's history that a veterinary cordon fence was removed – a conservation milestone. A further success was the commissioning by the government of the first Environmental Impact Assessment (EIA) of fences, largely paid for by British aid. The EIA team concluded that fences should be realigned to control the spread of cattle disease while opening up corridors for the Okavango's wildlife and maximising biodiversity and the health of the ecosystem. Its least favoured option (Map 2) was the extension of the foot-and-mouth disease-free area northwards from the Kuke, well into the greater Okavango ecosystem. This alignment would push the cattle export area zone right into Ngamiland, encircling the Delta with commercial cattle-raising country and disrupting wildlife movements. The government's adoption of the impact study's recommended option (Map 1) would be a major step forward.

The bite that protects

It is curious that, although the Okavango is designated a 'cattle-free zone', a long battle has been fought there against the tsetse, a small biting fly that carries trypanosomiasis. Wildlife is largely immune to the disease but livestock (especially cattle) readily succumbs, often with fatal results. The battle has continued since the 1950s, when a large amount of wildlife and huge tracts of forests were destroyed. Later, ground spraying with DDT was introduced, mostly replaced by aerial spraying in the 1980s.

The Delta enjoyed a period of grace for a decade when odour-baited traps were used instead of spraying. Over 50 000 traps were deployed, coloured black and blue to attract the fly and soaked in an insecticide that kills on contact. They are more environmentally friendly than aerial chemical spraying, but have proved difficult to maintain. Although aerial spraying was re-introduced for a two-year period from 2001, the Okavango Research Centre has at least been able to monitor its impact. Despite a low spray volume, a shocking 95 per cent decline in five major groups of insects was detected immediately after spraying.

Winds of change

The openness of the Botswana government in reconsidering policies regarding cattle fences in wildlife areas is encouraging. The country's vice president, Lt-Gen S K Ian Khama, first son of Botswana's first president, Sir Seretse Khama, is a respected conservationist and sits on a number of environmental boards including CI's. In contrast, commercial cattle farmers who exported to Europe in the past were invariably politicians who could write laws and promote subsidies that favoured cattle.

NGAMILAND EIA ON FENCES: PROPOSED OPTIONS

Map 1: EIA PREFERRED OPTION

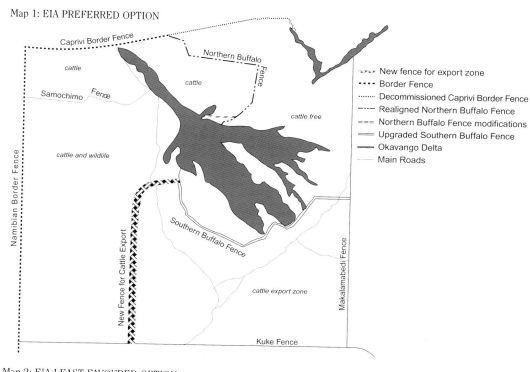

Map 2: EIA LEAST FAVOURED OPTION

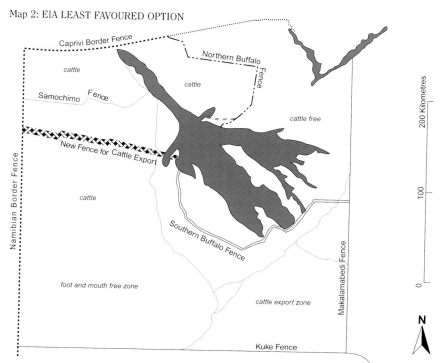

Botswana's priceless wildlife resource has increasingly gained attention internationally and at home. The formation of the 4 871-square-kilometre Moremi Wildlife Reserve in the 1960s was a bold step – the first wildlife sanctuary in southern Africa created by an African tribe on its own land and the only fully protected area in the Delta. Of Botswana's total land area, 17 per cent has been set aside as national parks and reserves. As these areas are not ecologically complete units, their size and shape dictated by other factors, it is important that corridors remain open so that animals can move freely within a network of protected areas. Botswana is one of the few countries in Africa where numbers of wild animals occur outside reserves.

Much of the country is divided into controlled hunting areas leased to hunting safari companies on an annual basis. Money from these concessions goes to the local Land Board, which is responsible for administering the area. Professional hunting is a big industry in Botswana, providing food and employment as well as revenue from licences and the sale of skins. In 1985 big-game hunting earned US$ 2 million in foreign exchange, growing to over US$ 5 million by 2001.

However, the Botswana government has placed a moratorium on hunting certain species in view of the decline in their numbers. The Okavango Lion Research Project recorded a lion population in the Delta of just over 1 000 animals (and fewer than 20 000 worldwide) in 2001. It led to a moratorium on the hunting of lions. In 2002 hunting sable and sitatunga antelopes was also banned. Predictably, this has caused dissension in the hunting fraternity, only some members of which supported the ban. More research is needed to clarify the issues and establish the status of species that are hunted.

Fortunately there has been more support for organisations that are linked to research. CI was one of the first non-governmental organisations to undertake aerial surveys of the Delta, in partnership with the University of Massachusetts and the Rufford Foundation. CI also conducted the first of a series of rapid biological assessments of the aquatic ecosystem, which have become an important baseline for the wetland.

There is still much to learn about the functioning of the Delta, but with an Okavango Research Centre now in place and the participation of other institutions and researchers a better picture of this remarkable ecosystem is beginning to emerge. Key to the protection of the Delta is the research carried out on species such as wild dog, elephant, zebra, cheetah, lion, hippo, crocodile and brown hyaena, among others. More than 13 years old, the Botswana Wild Dog Research Project is the world's longest running project on this endangered species.

An African giant, the rhinoceros, has been introduced, giving the Delta a full hand, and elephants are leading the way in a CI attempt to designate a 103 000 square mile transboundary conservation area encompassing Botswana, Angola, Namibia, Zambia and Zimbabwe.

Elephant migratory movements, recorded through satellite tracking, show the boundaries appropriate for such an area.

Many thousands of jobs are created directly through tourism, the biggest employer of any economic sector in northern Botswana. In 2002 the tourism sector netted $100 million. There has been a proliferation of all types of wildlife-based 'adventure' tourism, from elephant-back and horse safaris to four-wheel bike trips and mobile tented-camps. A new development is the opportunity for communities to start up, market and manage their own tourist operations in the Delta, sometimes in collaboration with established tour companies. In this way, about a third of the Okavango's designated tourism concessions have been awarded to local communities.

Empowering people through decision-making and securing a financial return enables them to become better custodians of their heritage. There are new developments in cultural tourism. For instance, with CI's assistance, over 500 Khwe Bushmen relocated to Gudigwa have developed a traditional village marketed by Wilderness Safaris. This is in contrast with their marginalisation in the last century and the recent evictions of Bushmen from the central Kalahari.

Momentum is gathering in an effort to conserve Botswana's valuable wildlife heritage. Large areas of land are designated 'wildlife management areas', where the commercial exploitation of wildlife can take place. They act act as buffer zones between protected areas and land settled by people and livestock. The EU has given Botswana grants of several million euro to upgrade its park system, and the Global Environment Facility has awarded a new grant for the Okavango river basin.

With the Okavango fences still in place, there are fears that the commercial cattle industry will continue to expand northwards. In the past policy has set cattle above wildlife. This bias is most clearly demonstrated by free veterinary fences, tax cuts and agricultural subsidies. While international attention has been drawn to the negative impacts of veterinary fences, plans currently sitting with cabinet could expand commercial cattle farming into the Okavango region to capture the valuable EU export market.

Noteworthy are the results of a study CI commissioned to compare the socio-economic costs and benefits of commercial cattle ranching, small-scale cattle farming and wildlife utilisation. In marginal areas of Ngamiland, without subsidies and tax concessions, commercial cattle ranching did not fare as well economically as traditional cattle farming methods, into which wildlife use is integrated. In prime areas such as the heart of the Delta, wildlife utilisation was, unequivocally, the most economical form of land use.

Can wildlife compete with cattle? The answer depends partly on where economic incentives are placed, but with the employment and revenues tourism generates in the Okavango and the increasing rarity and value of wildlife and wilderness, the answer could well be yes.

CHAPTER ELEVEN

Diamond Delta

t he last of the Okavango's waters some-times reach the river valley of the Boteti, dwarfed by high banks, heading across the Kalahari towards the edges of the Makgadikgadi pans. Nearby is Orapa, one of the richest diamond pipes in the world. For some 90 million years, it lay hidden beneath the flat-ness of the Kalahari's sands, unmarked by any striking features or change in topography.

Diamonds, the hardest natural substance known on earth, are formed of pure carbon, crystallised from the heat and stress of ancient volcanoes, held deep within volcanic pipes. Of the major diamond pipes to have been found in Africa, nearly half occur in Botswana. Diamonds are Botswana's greatest industry; this sparsely populated country is now the world's largest exporter of gem-quality diamonds.

The search for diamonds in the then largely uncharted territory of Botswana was initiated in 1955 by De Beers, the giant that markets most of the world's diamonds. Geologists, led by Gavin Lamont, began a search in the dry beds of sand rivers that exit the Kalahari to the south. For a long time they found nothing. Then, tantalisingly,

three small diamonds were found in the dry river bed of the Motloutse, a tributary of the Limpopo. The team searched the river, travelling towards its headwaters, seeking the pipe from which the gems had come. Their methodical prospecting revealed nothing.

Lamont's attention was caught by the theory of another great geologist, Alex Du Toit, who proposed the theory of continental drift and the breaking up of Gondwanaland. Du Toit had sug-gested that the tectonic rumblings that broke apart continents also caused the land to buckle and warp, creating rifts and diverted water courses. Was it possible that the upper Motloutse had been separated from its lower course by such warping, and that the true head-waters of the river lay on the opposite side of the slope they were prospecting?

The geologists began to search the vast Kalahari sand face to the north. Finally, years later, some tell-tale garnets, brought up by the activity of termites (which can tunnel hundreds of metres into the earth) were found near the Makgadikgadi pans. Within weeks a massive diamond pipe was discovered, running deep into the sands. It was called Orapa, after an isolated cattle post nearby. The find confirmed the existence of the Kalahari-Zimbabwe Fault, which had cut off the headwaters of the Motloutse at the point where diamonds were first discovered. It was the same fault that caused the ponding back of the northern rivers and thereafter the drying of Lake Makgadikgadi.

Diamonds and water schemes

Diamonds require great quantities of water to be extracted – ironic that the Orapa pipe should be located on the shores of an ancient lake long since dry. Although Orapa lies within 280 kilometres of the Delta, connected by the Boteti River valley, only occasionally does a tiny fraction of the Okavango's water reach it, leading to numerous attempts to increase the amount of flow. In the 1970s the Mopipi reservoir was developed to store the water of the Boteti River, thus draining the source of Lake Xau's water.

In the Delta the flow of the Boro was increased by dredging a stretch of the river. For some years the Mopipi reservoir filled, but in the drought years of the 1980s both the reservoir and Lake Xau dried up. The diamond mine once more resorted to boreholes to tap ancient groundwaters. In the fear that these would dry up long before the productive life of the mine had ended, eyes continued to turn to the waters of the Okavango.

Many attempts have been made to influence the flow of the Delta's waters, in hindsight most of them misguided. Hydrologists, governments, hunters, explorers and miners have all attempted at some time to open up new channels, build shallow dams and in one way or another to try to get at the waters.

One grandiose scheme proposed an aqueduct to take water from the Delta to Pretoria in South Africa. Another suggestion was a canal large enough to be navigable from the Panhandle to Botswana's capital city, a thousand kilometres to the south. A particularly wild proposal was the diversion of the Okavango and Chobe rivers into the Makgadikgadi pans to create a huge lake to be used for irrigated farming.

Fortunately for the Okavango, these ideas, which were based in the words of an economist on 'complete ignorance of topographic levels, unsound meteorological theory and at times very dubious arithmetic' remained untested. The soils around the southern Delta are hardly suited to irrigated farming. Some are very acidic, while others are highly alkaline. Moreover, intense evaporation brings to the surface salts that poison the soil.

The infamous Boro dredging

With the drying of the Boteti River and Mopipi reservoirs in the eighties, the Southern Okavango Development Water Project arose. Since it included a plan to dredge nearly 50 kilometres of the Boro River deep into the Delta to help increase water flow (to be stored in shallow dams along river valleys) it became popularly known as 'the Boro dredging project'. It was vehemently opposed both by conservationists and local communities, whose elders had seen the effects of so many failures in the past.

The project was proposed in several phases, the first the building of a series of reservoirs to supply water to Maun. Subsequently the flow of the Boro would be increased by dredging the river in a 100-metre-wide swath that would have taken out the riverine forest on either side. To carry two 70-tonne rigs needed to dredge the river a road on either side of the river would have to be constructed. The sludge would be deposited on the sides to create dam walls that would stop the water spilling the banks, thus preventing the natural flooding of the surrounding plains. Dredging would also cut through the Kunyere Fault, which ponds back the Delta's water. Small tributaries of the Boro would be blocked by a series of earthen dams.

The impact on large areas of seasonal floodplains, on water birds, animals, the breeding of fish, the access of people to wild foods and plants for medicine, building and weaving was mind-boggling. Roads would open up previously inaccessible areas of the Delta to heavy works machinery for construction work and maintenance. The Boro River, the only water access into the Delta from the south, would be destroyed as a natural river.

Tribal communities, conservationists and the international community were all vehemently opposed to the project. As a result of Green-

peace's threatened 'Diamonds are for Death' campaign against the diamond industry, the main beneficiaries of the project, De Beers publicly withdrew. Preparations continued, nevertheless, with contracts signed, machinery mobilised and people hired.

On 11 January 1991, just days before work on the project was due to begin, the Okavango community, guided by their regent chief and four prominent members known as the Front Line Four, invited a national political delegation to a 'kgotla' of over 700 tribesmen in Maun. The kgotla system is a part of Botswana's democratic tradition. It is the chief's court, and there is one in every village. Here the elders sit in a semi-circle, usually in chairs, while most of the crowd settles on the sand. Women also attend although they sit apart from the men. Everyone is allowed to speak for as long as they like; the chief and dignitaries are obliged to listen.

According to a tribesman: 'The kgotla is the most powerful tool of the tribe . . . those chairs in the sand under the tree or the posts that mark the chief's court – they have real power. This is the true forum for debate in Botswana.'

At the Boro dredging meeting, the people spoke. The Minister of Water had to endure a seven-hour, non-stop barrage from the Batawana people whose words were rousing and passionate. Some described the Delta as more precious than diamonds, a resource which, if cared for, could last forever. 'God made rivers meander for a reason,' they said, 'and they should not be straightened!' Some vowed to take up arms if the Delta were tampered with. The government delegation returned to the capital stunned by this impassioned opposition. The Minister of Water conferred with the President and the project was halted.

After a visit to Botswana at the invitation of the government, Greenpeace reiterated its strongly-held opinion that the Boro project should be shelved. A team of experts from the World Conservation Union (IUCN) was also asked to investigate and, after nearly a year's intensive work, concluded that the project was flawed. With substantial investment in the project, this was not good news for the government. But, to its credit, it cancelled the project and the Delta was left in peace.

Although there were many heroes in the saga, the Okavango communities stand out in their single-minded determination to stop the Boro dredging project. The international media rallied to the call of conservationists. Articles appeared in papers all over the world, raising the profile of the threat internationally. The Boro conservation success was a heartening combination of powerful forces: conservation watchdogs, community leaders and international media. And the government was remarkably democratic.

Halting the Boro project was more than just a victory for conservation. In the five drought-stricken years that followed – which would have blatantly revealed the flaws in the project – the harmful consequences of a water-stressed ecosystem would have been massive. As it was the Delta shrank and the Boro River, which becomes the Thamalakane River as it flows through Maun en route to the desert, dried up, not once but many times.

For a community that lives in a semi-desert, the loss of water was devastating. People suffered and their livestock died. Pods of hippos were stranded as the last pools of muddy water in the river that passes through Maun dried up. Again, however, the community rallied, arranging for water to be pumped to resupply hippos stuck in mud. An appeal was launched through South Africa's Carte Blanche television series, donations going towards feeding the starving hippos and keeping them alive until Botswana's Wildlife Department could begin the arduous task of trapping and relocating them to the Delta. Wildlife along a stretch of the Boro River that had been dredged 30 years before was not so lucky. The gracious yellow sycamore fig trees and reeds have died and fish no longer breed there.

Namibia's Master Water Plan

The Boro dredging was not the last time in recent years that upstream water withdrawal threatened the Okavango. Namibia's Master Water Plan scheduled for 2003 included the building of a 300-kilometre pipeline from the Okavango River to deliver water through the desert into an open canal, the water being destined for the capital city, Windhoek. It caused much concern among conservationists.

Two major issues were raised: one, the expected five-fold increase in Windhoek's demand for water in the next 20 years, which would raise water withdrawal to a level that could impact adversely on the Delta; the other, the preempting of the Okavango River Basin Commission (OKACOM) treaty between Angola, Namibia and Botswana, the first of its kind in Africa, on fair use of the Okavango river basin.

In 1996 Namibia was in the grips of a prolonged drought and its government announced emergency plans to build the pipeline. It was clear that no environmental impact assessment of the development had been planned. In response, Conservation International and the Kalahari Conservation Society founded a consortium of concerned environmental groups – the Okavango Liaison Group. Its first action was to call for an impact study. CI produced a 10-minute video news release, which was aired on all major television stations around the world. This brought international attention to the issue. However, good rains in late 1996 filled Namibia's dams and the project was postponed.

With plans for the pipeline only temporarily on hold, CI also commissioned a study entitled 'Meeting Namibia's water needs while sparing the Okavango' from a Namibian hydro-geologist and the International Rivers Network. The Liaison Group continued its work by raising awareness and building consensus among Okavango communities. In October 1999, the paramount chief of the Okavango communities,

Chief Tawana Moremi III, presented to the Namibian government the CI-commissioned report. 'There are many people,' he said, 'who, on a daily basis, sustain themselves from the river and Delta, and I am representing them.' He called on Namibia to abandon its water project just as Botswana had done a few years earlier.

All this activity paid off. The Namibia Water Corporation commissioned additional studies to re-examine Windhoek's water demands and to look at other water sources. The city's water requirements were found to be less critical than had previously been thought, and new groundwater sources were discovered. Plans for the pipeline were put on hold, and another crisis for the Okavango was narrowly averted.

A disaster in the making

Namibia at present is contemplating construction of a six- to eight-metre-high weir on the Okavango River just above Popa Falls in the Caprivi to divert water around the falls and generate hydro-electricity. Although there would be no water abstraction, the barrier would act as a dam and would affect the sediment flow of the river, which brings about 100 000 cubic metres of sand into the Delta every year.

The Delta is an alluvial fan fed by a vast network of river channels that distribute the water and sediments supplied by the Okavango River. These channels have a limited life as they quickly fill with sand, forcing a change in the pattern of water flow, thereby ensuring that the

Delta's ecosystem remains dynamic. Sediments causes rivers to be born and die remarkably quickly, creating a mosaic of vegetation types and water channels at different stages of development. Changing channels also help to keep the Delta's waters fresh despite massive evaporation, which leaves behind deposits of earth salts, which would otherwise accumulate to toxic levels, particularly on sands islands, are washed away by rain when a channel dries.

Removal of bedload sediment would occur with the construction of any dam along the upper reaches of the river. The full effect could take a hundred years to come into play, but would last forever. Professor T S McCarthy, the world's leading authority on the geology of the Okavango, has drawn attention to the long-term effects of sediment impoundment, and predicts a knock-on effect further downstream, resulting in a Delta that is less diverse and, in large sections, poisoned by the accumulation of toxic salts. His words are a dire warning.

Another threat to the ecology of the Delta looms large in the shape of a heavy industrial machine, costing a million US dollars, to clear river channels of papyrus. The work of clearing blocked channels is at present done by local people and creates much-needed employment. The introduction of a massive 'papyrus harvester' would pollute the waters, disrupt river channels and help spread salvinia, already a troublesome weed. Once again, forces are rallying to stop its introduction. Hopefully they will, again, succeed.

Sharing the Delta

All Africa's great swamps, from the Nile Sudd to the Okavango, have received the attention of those who wish to do something with the land or water beyond the natural order. The international character of the Okavango river basin and the competing demands for its water resources by the three countries that share it are a ready source of conflict.

In southern Africa, water is scarce. Its presence determines how well people survive and its absence leaves large areas uninhabitable. Angola, Namibia and Botswana all have access to the Okavango River, tempting them to harness its waters. As well as providing sustenance for a large indigenous community, the Delta is a valuable ecosystem and an important sanctuary for rare and endangered species. Given the ecological sensitivity of the area, the question arises: can the three countries concerned share it harmoniously and manage it together as a Transboundary Conservation Area?

A long-term solution may lie in finalisation of the work of the Okavango River Basin Commission. Attention will, it is hoped, be shifted from national gain to sustainable management of the Okavango's waters on four levels: at the regional level, the basin-wide management planning process is led by OKACOM; at the next level, governments are engaged in national planning activities such as Namibia's watersector analysis and Botswana's national wetlands policy; at the provincial level, regional institutions undertake water projects, for example the Namibian District Council's water-supply pipelines along the Delta; and at the local level, riparian towns and villages secure water for residents' daily use. One element is interwoven in these multiple layers – the people who live in the basin. Their widespread participation is a key to success.

Remarkably, the Okavango River is one of only 20 per cent of the world's rivers that are still wild. In other words it does not have any major works such as dams or large pipelines along its course. When, in 1996, the Botswana government designated the Delta an International Ramsar Site, it placed the area in the global arena. The Okavango is currently the largest Ramsar site in the world. Newer treaties, such as the World Heritage Sites Convention, would also help to give the Delta the protection that it needs from upstream neighbours and unexpected developments.

The Delta has faced some serious environmental challenges over the past decades. Conservation threats include water withdrawal, blanket spraying of pesticides, cattle encroachment, over-hunting and habitat fragmentation by fences. The natural world of the Okavango, nevertheless, remains remarkably intact. The ebb and flow of the waters continues, responding to cycles of drought and flood within the dynamics of a natural ecosystem. It is almost miraculous that this fragile wetland continues to exist unscathed.

Traps for wild creatures: long lines of gill nets (top) strung by fisherman across Okavango channels catch fish of all sizes indiscriminately, as well as water birds. On land, hundreds of kilometres of veterinary cordon fences (bottom) act as drift nets, trapping wildlife and blocking wilderness corridors.

New directions in tourism in the Okavango include elephant safaris (below) introduced by Randall Moore and quad biking (opposite middle), introduced by the legendary Jack Bousfield (Jack of the Pans). Unchartered Africa takes visitors to the arid wastes of the Makgadikgadi pans (opposite top). There is also the good old-fashioned safari adventure, author and child pictured here (opposite bottom) with Alistair Clark and Charlie Raitt.

Although upstream water withdrawals will always be a threat, the Okavango's waterways *(opposite)* remain unspoiled and relatively inaccessible. Derek Watts and the Carte Blanche crew *(this page, top)* film in the Okavango in 1991 at the height of the Boro dredging controversy. The Grootfontein Canal *(bottom)* is part of Namibia's proposed plan to draw water from the Okavango River to supply Windhoek and eastern Namibia via a 300-kilometre pipeline.

Old and new: a traditional Botswana village in the Makgadikgadi region (top) impresses with its beauty and simplicity. In the urban setting of the fast-growing frontier town of Maun, a Herero woman crosses a new tar road to visit the local store (bottom).

Members of Conservation International's National Advisory Council (from left) Mark Adcock, Charles Sheldon, Lt-Gen Fisher, Kgosi Moremi Tawana III, Karen Ross, Peter Sandenbergh, NAC chairman Jacob Nkate and CI-Botswana's director Innocent Magole at an Aquarap field site in the Delta (top). They are pictured with Jeff Randall and members of the crew of a BDF helicopter made available by Lt-Gen Fisher, seated in the craft (middle left) with Minister Jacob Nkate.

Professor Curtis and Jeff Burm of the University of Massachusetts have combined with CI to make aerial counts (bottom left) of large mammals in the Okavango. Dr Roger Bills (above) of the Grahamstown Institute of Ichthyology catches fish in an Aquarap survey.

Bibliography

GENERAL

Bannister, A. & Johnson, P., *Okavango – sea of land, land of water*, Struik Publishers, Cape Town, 1977.

Broadley, D.G. & Cock, E.V., *Snakes of Zimbabwe*, Longman Zimbabwe (Pty), 1975.

Campbell, A.C., *The guide to Botswana*, Winchester Press, Gaborone, 1980.

Coates Palgrave, K. *The trees of southern Africa*, Struik Publishers, Cape Town, 2002.

Kingdon, J. *East African mammals – an atlas of evolution in Africa*, vols I-VII, London, Academic Press, 1974.

Lee, R.B., *The Kung San – men, women and work in a foraging society*, Cambridge University Press, 1979.

Luard, N., *The last wilderness: a journey across the great Kalahari desert*, Elm Tree Books/Hamish Hamilton, London, 1981.

Miller, P., *Myths and legends of southern Africa*, T.V. Bulpin Publications (Pty) Ltd, Cape Town, 1979.

Newlands, G., *Biogeography and ecology of southern Africa*, ed. Werger, M.J.A., The Hague: Dr W. Junk, 1978.

Owens, M. & D., *Cry of the Kalahari*, Collins, London, 1985.

Roberts, A., *The birds of South Africa*. Revised edition by Maclean, Cape Town, 1996.

Roodt, V., *Trees & shrubs of the Okavango delta*, Shell Field Guide Series, Shell Oil, Botswana, 1998.

Shostak, M., *Nasa: the life and words of a !Kung woman*, Penguin, Harmondsworth, 1983.

Sillery, A., *Botswana: a short political history*, Methuen, London, 1974.

Skaife, S.H., *African insect life*, Struik Publishers, Cape Town, 1979.

Styen, P., *Birds of prey of southern Africa*, David Philip Publishers, Cape Town, 1982.

Tinley, K.L., *An ecological reconnaisance of the Moremi Wildlife Reserve, Botswana*, Johannesburg: Okavango Wildlife Society, 1966.

Tlou, T., *A history of Ngamiland – 1750 to 1906 – the formation of an African state*, Macmillan, Botswana, 1985.

Van der Post, Laurens, *The lost world of the Kalahari*, Penguin, Harmondsworth, 1962.

CONSERVATION INTERNATIONAL

Barnes, J., Cannon, J. & Morrison, K., *Economic returns to selected land uses in Ngamiland, Botswana*, Sept. 2000. (Typescript.)

Conservation International, 'Botswana rolls back fences for wildlife', *CI News from the Front*, 3:3 (1998).

Conservation International, *Final report of highwater Okavango Aquarap survey*, June 2000.

Hannah, L., Mittermeier, R., Ross, K., & Mast, R. 'New threats to the Okavango Delta, Botswana', *Oryx* 31 (1997), 86–89.

Ross, K. & Magole, I., 'Looking at the big picture: ecosystem management in mountains, watersheds and river basins', *Experiences in Southern Africa: The Okavango Delta and River Basin*, IUCN World Conservation Congress, Amman, Jordan, Oct. 2000.

Rothert, S., 'Meeting Namibia's water needs while sparing the Okavango Delta', *Publication series no. 2*, Joint publication of CI and IRN, CI Okavango Program, 1999.

SPECIALIST

Blomberg, G.E.D., 'Feeding and nesting ecology and habitat preferences of Okavango crocodiles', *Proceedings of the symposium on the Okavango Delta and its future utilisation*, Botswana Society, Gaborone, Botswana (1976).

Bowles, J., 'Current activities in tsetse control in Botswana', *Kalahari Conservation Society Newsletter* 4 (1984), 1–12.

Brown, L.H. & Seely, M., Abundance of the pygmy goose *Netta pus auritus* in the Okavango swamps, Botswana', *Ostrich* 44 (1973), 94.

Bruton, M. &Merron, G., 'The Okavango Delta – give credit where credit is due', *African Wildlife* 39:2 (1985), 59–63.

Calef, G., 'Mapping the movements of Botswana's elephants', *Kalahari Conservation Society Newsletter* 16 (1987).

Campbell, A.C., 'Comment on Kalahari wildlife and the Kuke Fence', *Botswana Notes and Records* 13 (1981), 111–18.

Carter, J.M., 'The development of wildlife management areas in Botswana', *Which way Botswana's wildlife?*, Proceedings of the symposium of the Kalahari Conversation Society, Gaborone, Botswana (1983), 63–73.

Child, G., 'The future of wildlife and rural land use in Botswana', *Proceedings, SARCCUS symposium on nature conservation as a form of land use*, Gorongosa National Park, Mozambique (1971), 78.

Child, G., 'Wildlife utilisation and management in Botswana', *Biol. Conserv.* 3 (1970), 18–22.

Collar, N.J. & Stuart, S.N., *Threatened birds of Africa and related islands: the ICBP/IUCN red data book* (Part One), Cambridge, 1985.

Ellery, W., Ellery, K., Rogers, K., McCarthy, T.S., & Walker, B., 'Vegetation, hydrology, and sedimentation processes as determinants of channel form and dynamics in the northeastern Okavango Delta, Botswana', *African Journal of Ecology* 31:25 (1993).

Comrie-Greig, J., 'The Eastern National Water Carrier – "killer canal" or life-giving artery? or both?' *African Wildlife* 40 (1986), 68–73.

Cooke, H.J.,'The origin of the Makgadikgadi Pans', *Botswana Notes and Records* 11 (1979), 37–42.

Cooke, H.J., 'The struggle against environmental degradation – Botswana's experience', *Desertificational Control*, UNEP, 8 (1983), 12.

Davies, J.E., *The history of tsetse fly control in Botswana*, Government of Botswana Department of Tsetse Fly Control, Gaborone, 1981.

Denbow, J.R., 'Early Iron Age remains from the Tsodilo Hills, north-western Botswana', *South African Journal of Science* 76:10 (1980), 474–75.

Douthwaite, R.J., Fox, P.J., Matthieson, P., & Russell-Smith, A., *The environmental impact of aerosols of Endosulfan applied to tsetse fly control in the Okavango Delta, Botswana*. Final report of the Endosulfan Monitoring Project, Overseas Development Administration, London, 1981.

Du Toit, A.L., in *The geology of South Africa*, (ed. Haughton, S.H., London: Oliver & Boyd, 1954).

Fowkes, J.D., *The contribution of the tourist industry to the economy of Botswana*. Report to the Kalahari Conservation Society, Gaborone, Feb. 1985.

Games, I., 'Feeding and movement patterns of the Okavango sitatunga', *Botswana Notes and Records* 16 (1984), 131–37.

Grove, A.T., 'Landforms and climatic change in the Kalahari', *The Geographic Journal* 135 (1969), 191.

Haacke, W.D., 'The herpetology of the southern Kalahari domain', *Proceedings of the symposium of the Kalahari ecosystem* (ed. de Graafe, G. and van Rensburg, D.J.), Pretoria (1984), 117–86.

Hedger, R.S., 'Foot-and-mouth disease in wildlife with particular reference to the African buffalo', *Wildlife Diseases* (1976), 235–43.

Huey, R.B. & Pianka, E.R., 'Natural selection for juvenile lizards mimicking noxious beetles', *Science* 195 (1977), 201–203.

Kalahari Conservation Society, Southern Okavango Integrated Water Development Project, *Kalahari Conservation Society Newsletter* (1986a), 11:8.

Leistner, O.A., *The plant ecology of the southern Kalahari*, Government of South Africa, Department of Agricultural Services, Botanical Memoir no. 38, Pretoria, 1967.

Liversedge, T.N., 'A study of Pel's fishing owl, *Scotopelia peli Bonaparte* 1850, in the Panhandle region of the Okavango Delta, Botswana', *Proceedings of the fourth Pan-African ornithological Congress* (1980): 291–99.

Lomba, R., 'The Lomba Archives', *The Lomba Foundation Report*, 26 pp, 1994.

Louw, G. & Seely, M., *Ecology of Desert Organisms*, New York: Longman, 1982.

Loveridge, J.P., 'Strategies of water conservation in southern African frogs', *Zoologica Africana* 11:2 (1976), 319–33.

McCarthy, J., Ellery, W., Rogers, K., Cairncross, M. & Ellery, K., 'The roles of sedimentation and plant growth in changing flow patterns in the Okavango,

Botswana', *South African Journal of Science*, 83, 579–584, 1994.

Maclean, G.L., 'Arid-zone adaptations in southern African birds', *Cimbebesia*, series A, 2:15 (March 1974), 163–76.

Meeuse, C., 'The pollination biology of *Nympheae*', *Proceedings of the second international congress of systematic and evolutionary biology*, University of British Columbia, Vancouver, 1980.

Merron, G., 'Fish research in the Okavango Delta', *Kalahari Conservation Society Newsletter* 11:9 (1986).

Michler, I., 'To snap or snipe?', *Africa Geographic* 10 (9):31-35, Oct. 2000.

Nel, J.A. & Bester, M.H., 'Communication in the southern bat-eared fox, *Otocyon m. megalotis*', Z. Saugetierkunde 48 (1983), 277–90.

Ngwamatsoko, K.T., 'Lessons for future livestock development projects in Botswana: wildlife resources considerations', *Proceedings of the symposium on Botswana's first Livestock Development Project and its future implications*, National Institute of Research, Gaborone, Botswana, June 1982, 143–63.

OKACOM, *Agreement between the governments of the Republic of Angola, the Republic of Botswana, and the Republic of Namibia on the establishment of a Permanent Okavango River Basin Commission (OKACOM)*, Windhoek, Namibia: Department of Water Affairs, Gaborone, Botswana: Department of Water Affairs, Angola., 1994).

Parris, R., 'The important role of Kalahari Pans', *African Wildlife* 24 (1970), 234–37.

Paterson, L., 'An introduction to the ecology and zoo-geography of the Okavango Delta', *Proceedings of the symposium on the Okavango Delta and its future utilisation*, Botswana Society, Gaborone (1976), 55–60.

Potten, D.H.,'Aspects of the recent history of Ngamiland', *Botswana Notes and Records* 8 (1974), 63–86

Scott Wilson Resource Consultants & the Environmental Development Group, *Environmental Assessment of Veterinary Fences in Ngamiland*, Final report prepared for the government of Botswana, 2000.

Shaw, P.A., 'A historical note on the outflows of the Okavango Delta system', *Botswana Notes and Records* 16 (1984), 128.

Silberbauer, G.B., *Report to the Bechuanaland government on the Bushman survey*, Government of Botswana (1965), 56–8.

Smith, P., '*Salvinia molesta*: an alien water weed in Botswana', *Kalahari Conservation Society Newsletter* 7 (1985), 10–12

Smith, P.A., 'An outline of the vegetation of the Okavango drainage system'. *Proceedings of the symposium on the Okavango and its future utilisation*, Botswana Society, Gaborone (1976), 93–112.

Taylor, C.R., 'The eland and the oryx', *Scientific American*, 220:1 (Jan. 1969).

The Namibian, 'Hands off our water, says Chief', front page headlines, Oct. 3, 2000.

Thompson, K., 'Ecology, management and utilisation of aquatic and semi-aquatic vegetation in the Okavango Delta, Botswana', *Technical report for UNDP project BOT/506*, UN/FAO Land and Water Development Division, 1974.

Tlou, T., 'The taming of the Okavango swamps – the utilisation of a riverine environment, 1750–1800', *Botswana Notes and Records* 6 (1972), 147–50.

United Nations, *Investigation of the Okavango Delta as a primary water resource for Botswana*, UNDP/FAO, Gaborone, Botswana, AG:DP/BOT/71/506, Technical report, vol. II, 1977.

Van Voorthuizen, E.G., 'The mopane tree', *Botswana Notes and Records*, 8 (1974), 227–30.

Veenendaal, E.M. & Opschoor, J.B., 'Botswana's beef exports to the EEC: economic development at the expense of a deteriorating environment', Institute of Environmental Studies, Free University, Amsterdam, 1985, typescript p. 46.

Williamson, D.T. & Williamson, J.E., 'Kalahari ungulate movement study', *Final report to Frankfurt Zoological Society and World Wildlife Fund* (1985), pp. 123 ff.

Wilson, B.H., 'Some natural and man-made changes in the channels of the Okavango Delta', *Botswana Notes and Records* 15 (1983), 138.

Index & Species List